THE
SAVVY
INVESTOR'S
GUIDE FOR
CRAZY TIMES

T0289429

MAKING YOUR
MILLIONS
IN REITs

GABRIEL YAP

Marshall Cavendish
Business

Published by Marshall Cavendish Business
An imprint of Marshall Cavendish International

A member of the
Times Publishing Group

Other Marshall Cavendish Offices:
Marshall Cavendish Corporation, 800 Westchester Ave, Suite N-641, Rye Brook, NY 10573, USA •
Marshall Cavendish International (Thailand) Co Ltd, 253 Asoke, 16th Floor, Sukhumvit 21 Road,
Klongtoey Nua, Wattana, Bangkok 10110, Thailand • Marshall Cavendish (Malaysia) Sdn Bhd,
Times Subang, Lot 46, Subang Hi-Tech Industrial Park, Batu Tiga, 40000 Shah Alam, Selangor
Darul Ehsan, Malaysia

Marshall Cavendish is a registered trademark of Times Publishing Limited

National Library Board Singapore Cataloguing-in-Publication Data

Name(s): Yap, Gabriel.
Title: Making your millions in REITs : the savvy investor's guide for crazy
    times / Gabriel Yap.
Description: Singapore : Marshall Cavendish Business, [2021]
Identifier(s): OCN 1200833415 | ISBN 978-981-49-2825-0 (paperback)
Subject(s): LCSH: Real estate investment trusts.
Classification: DDC 332.63247--dc23

Printed in Singapore

Teach like there is no better LEAP
Learn like there is no better REAP
Invest like there is no better REIT
Strive like there is no better HIGH
Love like there is no better TOMORROW

DISCLAIMER

The author is not an attorney, accountant or financial advisor. All the information presented in this book is done so for educational purposes only. The information provided in this book is not legal or financial advice and it is not intended to be a substitute for legal or financial advice that should be provided by your own attorney, accountant and/or financial advisor. Although care has been taken in preparing the information provided in this book, GCP Global (wholly-owned subsidiary of GCP Management Holdings Pte Ltd), GCP Management Holdings Pte Ltd and the author cannot be held responsible for any errors or omissions, and GCP Global, GCP Management Holdings Pte Ltd and the author accept no responsibility and liability whatsoever for any loss or damage that a reader may incur. Always seek financial and/or legal counsel relating to your specific circumstances as needed for any and all questions and concerns you may have.

Past performance is no guarantee of future results. All REITs investments involve a risk of loss. There is no assurance that a REITs investment will be profitable. Not all REITs investments are suitable for all investors as each investor is different. If there are any doubts, advice should be sought from an independent financial advisor.

While the publisher and the author have used their best efforts and due diligence in preparing this book, including taking all necessary steps to ascertain that all relevant information is correct and accurate to the best of their knowledge, no warranties are made about the completeness, reliability and accuracy of the information presented in this book. Any implied warranties of merchantability or fitness for a particular purpose are specifically disclaimed. No warranty may be created or extended by sales representatives or written sales materials. The thoughts and strategies contained in this book may not be suitable for any individual reader's situation. A professional should always be consulted as appropriate. Neither the publisher nor the author or any related companies shall be liable for any loss of profit or any other commercial damages, including but not limited to special, incidental, consequential or other damages.

CONTENTS

FOREWORD

"REIT Guru" would be an apt middle name for Gabriel. My first encounter with Gabriel occurred after I became the Chief Executive at ESR-REIT. That conversation left an indelible impression on my team and I, as he was one of the few people who asked critical, thought-provoking and pointed questions few people would dare to ask. My conversations with Gabriel since then have been illuminating – I always take away an important insight from his perspective which has been useful in my investor interactions and how my team and I develop our strategic directions for ESR-REIT.

I am always amazed at how he is able to make investing fun and simple for people to learn from him. Breaking down seemingly complex transactions into simple, easy to understand, layman scenarios and, importantly, how to execute and leverage on the opportunities presented. Even though he keeps up a hectic schedule, Gabriel always finds time to connect with people, regularly sending articles he's read that he thinks my team and I will find insightful. He is a dedicated educator at heart.

Over the years, numerous analysts and pundits and other experts have produced a myriad of articles, blog posts, books and podcasts on investing in REITs. But only a select few promise to truly move the needle in practice, and even fewer still advocate the importance of sensible long-term investing.

So here are three things you will learn from Gabriel:

THE INVESTING JOURNEY IS FULL OF TWISTS AND TURNS

The first thing people learn from Gabriel, of course, is why choose REITs. Given many investors are generally eager to generate both value and growth in their portfolios, they direct capital to less-volatile investments such as REITs, which are expected to yield stable income and long-term capital appreciation. But now there's a roadblock in the investing journey: as COVID-19 continues to ravage global markets, how does one evaluate REITs in the middle of a worldwide disruption the likes of which we have never seen? How do you determine a good REIT to invest in?

COVID-19 has rewritten the rules of real estate. Investors have reluctantly accepted the fact that businesses are unlikely to return to "normal" anytime soon. Concerns, whether shopping, work or leisure will still be the same and the ability of tenants to sustain their operations once the pandemic subsides has weighed heavily on everyone's mind. These questions are likely to prompt investors to be more astute in their investments. Some may direct their capital away from riskier assets, while others are likely to morph into bargain hunters.

That's where Gabriel's REITs investing framework comes in handy. It is nimble enough that people can use it anytime, even in shifting market dynamics and changing risk appetites. The framework emphasises being prepared, and that means being diverse when it comes to investing in REITs.

FUNDAMENTALS ARE IMPORTANT

The pandemic spotlights issues such as business continuity by exposing and accentuating structural weaknesses in fundamentals that companies have long overlooked or neglected. Similarly, companies with healthy indicators such as strong operating balance sheet metrics, diversified portfolio, robust capital structure and a good management team are more likely to withstand shocks in the global economy. The same can be applied to REITs.

In this book, Gabriel has included several approaches towards REITs valuation where investors can significantly minimise risk by filtering out risky REITs with poor fundamentals from the outset.

LOOK OUT FOR OPPORTUNITIES

The pandemic accelerated trends that were already visible even before infection rates started creeping up. The most obvious is the rise of e-commerce. Technology has upended real estate globally. The surge in online shopping has been a boon to warehouses and data centres. For example, evolving consumer behaviour has changed the way investors are looking at industrial REITs as they pivot towards a more defensive portfolio. Crisis periods often offer excellent opportunities to profit. And the current REIT market presents the best classroom.

Gabriel is not afraid to bring across sentiments from the investing community and pose the hard questions to us as REIT managers. This is one of his most admirable qualities.

It is from this rare breed of REIT advocates – grounded in experience and success in practice – that this book truly enlightens.

I hope you will enjoy his insights as much as I did.

Adrian Chui
Chief Executive Officer & Executive Director
ESR Funds Management (S) Ltd

PREFACE

Having navigated crises like the 1987 and 1989 stock market crash, the 1997–1998 Asian Financial Crisis, the Dot-com bubble and the 2007–2009 Global Financial Crisis successfully, it became crystal clear to me that how investments and finance are taught in universities and what the smart and sharp investor should be equipped with psychologically, mentally and with the necessary financial skills, can make a huge difference to an investor's wealth – you can either let a crisis get to you or capitalize on it to make your millions.

I have been lucky and thank the Lord for being able to make my millions from past crises and REITs to retire in 2009 in my early 40s. As a form of thanksgiving, I have continued to teach but with a difference – since 2010, I have been donating a portion of the proceeds from teaching to various charities. After 31 years of teaching, I have more than 8,000 student investors from all over Asia who attend our REITs, Technology and Investment classes regularly.

I have written this book to encapsulate what we have taught – betting big in times of crises and multiplying wealth through REITs, Technology and Disruption Innovation stocks. In this book, as in our investment classes, we focus on how to invest in REITs to become potential millionaires and how to protect and grow one's wealth, more so after the COVID-19 pandemic which sent REITs and capital markets reeling. The sell-off has been one of the most ruthless ever, however, every crisis creates a new opportunity for REIT investors to make and mint new wealth – if you know how. This book delves deep into that.

Whether you are new to the world of REITs or already a sophisticated investor, you will gain great insights and gain a firmer understanding of REITs investment strategy and tactical allocation changes that vary with market changes.

The first-time or beginner REIT investor will benefit from a structured approach from the book as it covers issues in depth in understandable terms, including the different levels of REIT investing and provides real-life examples of REITs. It teaches the reader in clear terms how to analyze REITs via several approaches to conserve and grow one's wealth.

To give sophisticated investors an edge, I share passionately on how to navigate the ups and downs of the REITs market as it moves with the vagaries of interest rate changes, expectations and events that shape the REITs market. I have also incorporated some of my experiences as I built my stakes to become one of the top 20 shareholders in some of the REITs.

As I am excited and see a great future in the development of REITs in jurisdictions like Singapore, India and China in the future, this book has a detailed section on how Singapore's REIT market grew over different time periods – growth pangs, like the growth of a child, are natural. The sagacious investor will know how best to harness the spills and thrills, so as to come out thrilled all the time.

Readers will be guided on what to watch out for in the REIT market moving ahead. Areas like Mergers of REITs and Acquisitions of both local and foreign assets to gain geographical advantage will be covered with live examples of deals and guided by my template on how to analyze and scrutinize a good or bad deal.

The book will also provide details on the sell signals that I look for in selling my strategic stakes in REITs before the REIT price plunges. Not only does it teach investors on what and when to buy, it also touches on the other more important skills of Taking Profits and Cutting Your Losses.

If the past is a prologue to the future, you, the sagacious REIT investor, will be well-guided in this book to stay sharp and smart, and to continue making your millions in REITs.

Gabriel Yap
December 2020

Chapter 1

WHAT THE PERSPICACIOUS REIT INVESTOR SHOULD LEARN FROM THE COVID-19 CRISIS

This time, it is different!

The COVID-19 Pandemic pushed the global economy into a recession of historic proportions and halted the longest-lasting equity bull market. As infections spread globally and exponentially, economic activity collapsed and came to a standstill. Then policy makers responded and markets rebounded strongly. The COVID-19 crisis provides a real-time case study of what happens to the income of Real Estate Investment Trusts (REITs) and their flow-through impact on the REITs' dividends during times of unprecedented stress. This directly challenges the long-held perception among investors that REITs are safe vehicles for investments as they are mandated to pay out at least 90% of their taxable income as dividends to achieve tax transparency. The severe market sell-down, in terms of the speed and magnitude, was indeed fast and furious and unprecedented.

For the first time ever, S-REITs collapsed 367.98 points which was a humongous 37.91% as the FTSE REIT Index crashed from 970.62 on Wednesday, 19 February 2020 to 602.64 on Monday, 23 March 2020, over a period of just 22 market days! This fierce sell-off was the worst ever in S-REIT history and exceeded the previous record of October 2008, where in the throes of the Global Financial Crisis (GFC), 34.67% in value was wiped off in a single month.

As a comparison, S-REITs sold off 22.5% over a period of 77 market days (about 4x longer than 22 days) during the 2015 Taper Tantrum sell-off. Of course, the worst-ever sell-off in S-REITs was during the GFC where the FTSE REIT Index collapsed 74.67%, but it was over 13 months or 266 market days.

The ferociousness of the sell-off was very much attributed to the fear of the unknown. In this case, it is the coronavirus that is the known factor, but the unknown effects range from how long will this pandemic last, when will infections peak and how many deaths will subsequently follow. Investors do not like uncertainty and will certainly sell first and ask questions later. The sell-off was akin to "throwing the baby out with the bath water", not dissimilar to previous sell-offs.

How the smart REIT investor positions his or her portfolio in this time of crisis is key in making a fortune. After all, S-REITs' 37.91% fall to 602.64 on Monday, 23 March 2020 inked it as the 2nd largest fall in S-REITs' 19-year history since the S-REIT market started in 2002. And every crisis creates its own opportunity for the sagacious REIT investor.

In comparison, the US REIT market lost 39.95% or a market value of US$884.1 billion. Globally, equities lost US$26.1 trillion in market capitalization and US stocks alone lost $11.8 billion in market capitalization during the sell-off.

Personally, I have navigated many crises like the 1987 and 1989 stock market crashes, 1998 Asian Financial Crisis and 2008 Global Financial Crisis. Crises are times when fundamentals and technical analysis take a back seat and experience takes the front seat. Investors and traders have to contend with swings from Fear to Greed and vice versa, sometimes in a matter of seconds.

Financial markets have always seen the struggle between order and chaos. For the last decade, financial markets have been relatively calm and orderly and prices have gone up after each correction. COVID-19 has thrown many of our lives into chaos and businesses that were doing just fine a few months back, all of a sudden are facing an existential crisis.

What I have learned from past crises is that chaos in markets not only brings about destruction. But out of this crisis and chaos will emerge new businesses and sow the seeds of the next Amazon. After all, Amazon nearly went under during the Global Financial Crisis and has emerged as a force to reckoned with. The challenge for investors is to survive the current crisis and chaos and identify and position into the winners that will emerge out of this mess. Therein, is the way to multiplying your wealth, as it has happened in the past, will happen now, and also in the future.

What I have learned from past crises is: Crises are the best learning experiences for the smart investor and the best time to multiply one's wealth. These are some of the invaluable lessons that emerged from the COVID-19 Pandemic and are likely to change the REIT investment landscape going forward:

HOW SAFE ARE REIT DIVIDENDS?

REIT dividend yields may be attractive. Many REITs like to show their dividend yield compared to equities, government 10-year bond yields, the Central Provident Fund rate and Fixed Deposit rates in their various quarterly or half-year results. But dividend yield is meaningless if the dividend behind it is not sustainable or withheld due to COVID-19, as many REIT investors came to experience in this COVID-19 crisis when REITs released their 1Q2020 results.

The contractual nature of rental revenue from leases has enabled REITs to pay steady dividends to investors, even during most economic recessions. Historically, as long as REIT managers do not finance the REIT's growth with excessive levels of leverage, the bond-like cash flows of dividends will continue without much interruption to investors. However, that changed for S-REIT investors with the COVID-19 crisis.

Prior to that, the 2007-2008 Global Financial Crisis (GFC) that precipitated the 2008-2009 economic recession was the preamble that severe economic and market stresses can jeopardize REIT dividends. In the US, over two-thirds of all REITs cut or suspended their DPU in order to conserve cash. According to NAREIT, REIT returns were a dismal negative 37.7% in 2008, before rebounding to a positive 28.0% in 2009. Despite widespread dividend cuts, in 2008, REITs underperformed the S&P500 by only 73 basis points and outperformed equities by 153 basis points in 2009.

The rash of dividend cuts by REITs during the 2008-2009 recession was similar to that of the REITs that slashed their dividends in the wake of the savings and loan crisis in the 1980s. In both instances, a broad liquidity crisis translated into dividend cuts for the majority of REITs. Not surprisingly, the REITs that did not cut or suspend their dividends were the ones with lower levels of debt, and also those with little debt maturing during the crisis years.

The key aspect of Dividend Safety takes centre stage during the COVID-19 crisis. There are a few key factors that investors should pay special attention to in determining Dividend Safety which we will delve into, in great detail in Chapters 4 and 5.

LESSON LEARNED

REIT dividend yields may be defensive and attractive. However, they are meaningless if the dividends behind them are not sustainable or withheld due to COVID-19, as many REIT investors came to experience during the COVID-19 crisis when REITs released their 1Q2020 results.

THE RIGHT SECTOR PICKS & REITS SELECTION IS KEY TO WEALTH GENERATION
COVID-19's Impact on Hospitality REITs

Both the hospitality and retail REITs were literally in the eye of the storm of the COVID-19 crisis. The COVID-19 pandemic has plunged both sectors into uncharted operating territories from mid-March and is expected to play out in full through 2Q2020 and possibly 2H2020.

For instance, at newly-listed ARA US Hospitality Trust, gross revenue and net property income (NPI) fell sharply below the company's forecasts by 24.5% and 68.2% when it delivered its 1Q2020 results at US$31.7 million and US$3.6 million, respectively. Frasers Hospitality Trust which owns assets in places ranging from Kobe, Japan to Sydney, Australia, also reported a sharp 41.5% decline in revenue to $20.2 million and a sharper 52% drop in NPI to $12.1 million. Shareholders suffered a terrible blow as the REIT retained $25.3 million in its 1H2020 dividend distributions in anticipation of continued weak operating performance and to support one of its recently acquired properties, the Novotel Hotel Melbourne on Collins which is not under master lease protection.

WORST-HIT REITS 1Q2020	Share Price 31/12/2019	Share Price 31/03/2020	Price Change	% Change
Eagle Hospitality Trust	$0.545	$0.137	-$0.408	-74.86%
ARA Hospitality Trust	$0.870	$0.345	-$0.525	-60.34%
United Hampshire	$0.800	$0.320	-$0.480	-60.00%
CDL HT	$1.620	$0.800	-$0.820	-50.62%
Lippo Malls	$0.225	$0.117	-$0.108	-48.00%
Far East Hospitality Trust	$0.740	$0.410	-$0.330	-44.59%
Frasers Hospitality Trust	$0.710	$0.395	-$0.315	-44.37%
Landlease REIT	$0.930	$0.520	-$0.410	-44.09%
ESR REIT	$0.530	$0.300	-$0.230	-43.40%
Ascott REIT	$1.330	$0.790	-$0.540	-40.60%

All of the six hospitality REITs were in the 10 worst-hit REITs for 1Q2020

Hospitality REITs bore the brunt of the sell-off. There are six hospitality REITs listed on SGX and all of them were in the worst-10 performing REITs for 1Q2020 list. The losses ranged from 74.86% for Eagle Hospitality Trust (which is still suspended as this book goes to print) to 40.60% for Ascott REIT. While newly-listed ARA US Hospitality REIT lost 60.34% in value, long-listed CDL Hospitality Trust also lost 50.62% in value.

Interestingly, this sell-off also showed that REITs like CDL Hospitality, Ascott REIT and Far East Hospitality which have some of their incomes underwritten by their master lessors or sponsors, were as badly affected as those without. Far East Hospitality has a high 72% fixed rent/stable income component, CDL Hospitality has 36% while Ascott REIT has 30%. As of end-June 2020, hospitality REITs prices are still down by more than 25%, the sharpest among all REIT sectors, while industrial REITs like ESR REIT have recovered by 32%.

Hospitality REITs typically have geographically diversified assets relative to other REIT sectors. It was traditionally a strength as market dynamics of one geographical area may outweigh the weakness in others, a strength that Ascott REIT has repeatedly pointed out. However, with the pandemic and possible global recession, this off-setting is clearly negated.

With the closure of country borders and restriction of travel, occupancies fell like ten-pins which together with falling Average Daily Rates, led to severe erosion of the Revenue Per Available Room (RevPAR). The high fixed cost nature of the hospitality sector, comprising operating, administrative and financing costs had come home to roost.

Sector rotation is an investment strategy that consists of moving money from one sector to another to outperform the market. Over time, an economy moves through periods and bouts of expansion and contraction. Economic growth and demand-supply dynamics typically benefit certain sectors, known as cyclical sectors during an expansion while less economically sensitive sectors perform more defensively during economic contractions.

For instance, among the top-10 best performing REITs for 2017, four of the REITs were in the Office sector. They were CapitaCommercial Trust (now known as CapitaLand Commercial Trust), Suntec REIT, Mapletree Greater China (now known as Mapletree North Asia or Mapletree NAC, which owns office properties in China and Japan) and Keppel REIT. The Office sector enjoyed strong momentum in economic growth and favourable demand-supply dynamics which subsequently saw increases in spot rentals and falling occupancies.

For the smart and sharp REIT investor, profits come from both capital gains and dividends. COVID-19 Crisis brought to the forefront that avoiding capital losses in a crisis sell-off is equally important as buying correctly when you position your REITs investment portfolio. It illustrated what we have been teaching for the past 31 years: Rock-bottom prices present themselves, but you need to avoid the sectors and REITs that will drag your portfolio down to be able to take advantage of good and profitable bottom-picking in the other sectors.

LESSON LEARNED

For the smart and sharp REIT investor, profits come from both capital gains and dividends. COVID-19 Crisis brought to the forefront that avoiding capital losses in a crisis sell-off is as important as positioning your REITs investment portfolio. Highly susceptible sectors like Hospitality which can result in huge losses should have been avoided going into the crisis.

COVID-19's Impact on Retail REITs

Retail properties derive their value from footfall and tenant sales in addition to their convenient location factor. A combination of all these factors have driven retail values up in the past few decades. In addition, hanging out in malls is a favourite pastime with locals as you can literally go crazy in land-scarce Singapore, cooped up in small apartments which are mainly Housing and Development Board flats (which house more than 80% of the population) of typical size under 90 square metres.

On April Fools' Day, many REIT investors may have felt like fools when SPH REIT became the first S-REIT to slash its DPU in its latest quarterly results due to the anticipated challenges that COVID-19 would pose. The COVID-19 pandemic subsequently led to temporary closure of shops deemed non-essential and social distancing measures introduced caused most malls to become "ghost" malls for the months of April and May 2020. Even before COVID-19, there were already pockets of weakness in the retail sector which saw the departure of a mix of large fashion chains and local brands.

The malls had been able to reposition by welcoming activity-based tenants such as cooking classes, craft workshops, education and tuition centres, gyms and virtual reality arcades which thrive on group-based activities. The social distancing measures put in place to prevent and lower the spread of COVID-19 is certainly going to affect footfall and tenant sales going forward, even after the re-opening of the economy.

RETAIL REITS	Share Price	Share Price	Price	%
	31/12/2019	31/03/2020	Change	Change
CapitaLand Mall Trust	$2.460	$1.790	-$0.670	-27.24%
Frasers Centrepoint Trust	$2.810	$2.240	-$0.570	-20.28%
Mapletree Commercial Trust	$2.390	$1.830	-$0.560	-23.43%
SPH REIT	$1.070	$0.770	-$0.300	-28.04%
Lendlease Global REIT	$0.930	$0.520	-$0.410	-44.09%
Starhill Global REIT	$0.725	$0.435	-$0.290	-40.00%

There is a clear disparity in performance in retail REITs. A retail REIT is as resilient as the mix of tenants it has in the malls that it owns.

Not surprisingly, the stronger of the retail REITs, namely Frasers Centrepoint Trust, Mapletree Commercial Trust (MCT) and CapitaLand Mall Trust lost between 20.28%–27.24% of their value in 1Q2020. The other retail REITs, Lendlease REIT and Starhill Global REIT lost 44.09% and 40.00% in value, respectively.

The disparity in performance among retail REITs is clear to the sharp and smart REIT investor. A retail REIT is as resilient as the mix of tenants that it has in the malls that it owns. Some malls like VivoCity owned by MCT did not see any valuation downgrade. In fact, VivoCity was able to maintain its valuation at $3.262 billion or $3,031 per square foot in its 1Q2020 results. Subsequently, due to lower rentals assumed by its valuers, it had a 3.5% devaluation while maintaining its cap rate, in its latest 3Q2020 results announced in October 2020. In reality, VivoCity has been able to continuously post positive NPI growth year-on-year since it started operations on 7 October 2006. Yes, even 14 years after the mall opened.

Portfolio Valuation

mapletree commercial

	Portfolio valuation held steady at S$8.9 bil				
	Valuation as at 31 March 2020[1]			Valuation as at 31 August 2019	Valuation as at 31 March 2019
	S$ million	S$ per sq ft NLA	Cap Rate	S$ million	
VivoCity	3,262.0	3,031 psf	4.625%	3,262.0	3,200.0
MBC I	2,198.0	1,287 psf	Office: 3.90% Business Park: 4.95%	2,193.0	2,018.0
PSA Building	791.0	1,505 psf	Office: 4.00% Retail: 4.85%	786.0	763.0
Mapletree Anson	762.0	2,317 psf	3.50%	762.0	728.0
MLHF	347.0	1,608 psf	3.90%	347.0	330.0
Sub-total	7,360.0			7,350.0	7,039.0
MBC II	1,560.0	1,317 psf	Business Park: 4.90% Retail: 4.75%	1,550.0[2]	-
MCT Portfolio	8,920.0[3]			8,900.0	7,039.0

1. The valuation for VivoCity was undertaken by Savills Valuation and Professional Services (S) Pte. Ltd., while the valuations for MBC I and II, PSA Building, Mapletree Anson and MLHF were undertaken by CBRE Pte. Ltd.
2. Refers to the Agreed Property Value
3. Given current market conditions and on a goodwill basis, the Manager will charge the base management fees for FY20/21 based on the prevailing asset value or new valuation, whichever is lower

MCT's valuation in 1Q2020 results

Whilst all malls are hit with the same problems of closure of "non-essential services", social distancing measures and high probability of lower rental renewals, not all malls are affected the same way. The best retail REITs will differentiate themselves from the rest and still outperform during a crisis. They will also most likely outperform further in the years ahead. This is a great lesson that REIT investors should take note of, from the COVID-19 Pandemic sell-off.

LESSON LEARNED

Whilst all malls are hit with the same problems of closure of "non-essential services", social distancing measures and high probability of lower rental renewals, not all malls are affected the same way. The smart REIT investor should know that a retail REIT is as resilient as the mix of tenants in the malls that it owns, nothing more, nothing less. The best retail REITs will differentiate themselves from the rest and outperform in the years ahead.

COVID-19's Impact on Industrial REITs

On the other hand, industrial REITs have proven to be more resilient. COVID-19 amplified the critical role that supply chain management, logistics and e-commerce play. The share prices of the larger industrial REITs like Ascendas REIT, Mapletree Logistics Trust (MLT), and Mapletree Industrial Trust (MIT), recovered to within 10–15% of their pre-crisis prices during the rebound that followed the crash. Keppel DC REIT which own data centres, actually saw its share price challenge its pre-crisis price within four weeks of the low reached on 23 March 2020.

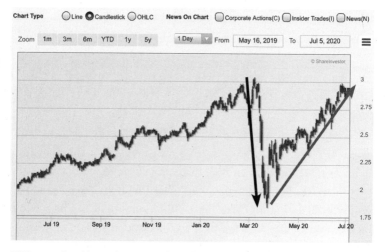

MLT recovered quickly to within 10-15% of its pre-crisis levels during the rebound. Source: ShareInvestor

Most of the industrial REITs subsequently reported that most of their tenants cater to industry sectors that are deemed essential and were allowed to operate. Not surprisingly, when the industrial REITs reported their 1Q2020 results or Business Updates, most did not see the need to withhold DPU as only a small proportion of their tenants actually asked for rental deferrals.

Keppel DC REIT, MLT and Ascendas REIT did not withhold DPU. MIT withheld a small sum of $6.6 million as it has exposure to small and medium-sized enterprises (SMEs), comprising 50–55% of its tenant base as compared to Ascendas REIT where SMEs make up just 20–25% of its tenant mix.

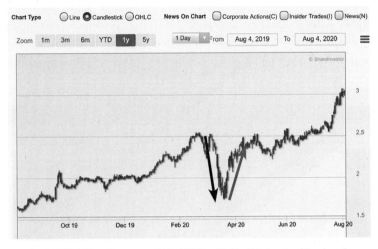

Keppel DC REIT challenged its pre-crisis high of $2.50 to $2.55 within 4 weeks of the rebound.
Source: ShareInvestor

The Most Resilient REITs vs The Worst-Performing REITs during COVID-19

Why are doctors so confident in being able to differentiate between a heart attack and a headache? This is because they extensively study the symptoms of both. Similarly at GCP Global, we have trained our student investors to avoid Value Traps for the past three decades by extensively studying the early symptoms and issuing warnings way in advance on REITs.

Heart attacks and strokes, the seizure can come anytime and send the victims into sharp pain and possible convulsions. Similarly, the COVID-19 Crisis was another episode that highlighted that there are Good REITs and there are Not-so-good REITs. During a crisis, there will be convulsions which can result in sharp pain in an investment portfolio, but the Strong REITs are the ones that rebound the fastest while the Not-so-strong REITs will rebound the least and slowest. We will cover the characteristics of a Good Reit in Chapters 4 and 5 and highlight Value Traps in subsequent chapters.

As in Table 1, the worst-five performing REITs lost between 48.00% to 74.86% of their value during the COVID-19 Pandemic sell-down. Most of the hospitality REITs including Eagle Hospitality Trust, ARA Hospitality Trust, CDL HT and Lippomalls were some of the REITs that we had told our student investors to AVOID in our various quarterly REIT classes, monthly write-ups and symposiums prior to 2019.

MOST RESILIENT	Share Price	Share Price	Price	%
Jan - Apr 2020	31/12/2019	30/04/2020	Change	Change
Keppel DC REIT	$2.08	$2.35	$0.27	12.98%
Mapletree Logistics Trust	$1.74	$1.80	$0.06	3.45%
Ascendas REIT	$2.97	$2.97	$0.00	0.00%
Parkway Life REIT	$3.32	$3.30	($0.02)	-0.60%
Mapletree Industrial Trust	$2.60	$2.55	($0.05)	-1.92%

Top-five best performing REITs during the COVID-19 crisis

In contrast, the top-five performing REITs held on to their capital values during the COVID-19 sell-off. In fact, Keppel DC REIT and MLT even exceeded their pre-crisis price levels by end-April 2020. All five REITs were what we had shared extensively in our various quarterly REIT classes, monthly write-ups and symposiums prior to 2019. Many of these REITs have been our favourites for a long time.[1]

Most of the smaller industrial REITs held back dividends as their exposure to SME clients tend to be higher. It became clear that properties leased to high-quality tenants, especially to MNCs and blue-chip tenants in essential services presented the least risk of rental default or postponement. They are also more likely to fulfil long-term leases. Going behind who are the tenants and stress-testing their financial health take centre stage in this crisis as that underlies whether these tenants would be able to withstand this financial grind. It brings forth what we have been teaching in our REITs classes in the past 31 years – the financial veracity of the

---

1   "Picking S-REIT Winners For 2020", GCP Global, 8/2/2020, https://gcpglobalsg.wixsite.com/gcpglobal/post/picking-s-reit-winners-for-2020. "Singapore REITs – Replete With Splendour," GCP Global, 12/1/2020, https://gcpglobalsg.wixsite.com/gcpglobal/post/singapore-reits-replete-with-splendour.

tenants is key in determining a REIT's safety of rental income. The safety of the rental income will then translate into the safety of the DPU for investors.

Summary

Post-COVID-19, the key factors to watch in sectors and REITs are income flows, rental reversions, vacancies, lease maturities, gearing, cost of fund and interest cover. Maintaining cash flow visibility to thrive and still pay unit holders, balanced against the need for capital retention, are the new hallmarks.

It is clear therefore for REIT investors, that the REITs that have been more resilient and will do better in the coming recovery, after perhaps a quarter or two of really bad economic results, will be in the more specialized niche areas of data centres and healthcare. The larger and diversified industrial REITS with defensive industry mix that can bolster their balance sheets quicker, will also be the more resilient REITs.

As the COVID-19 Crisis sell-down has shown, REITs are not homogeneous. In fact, the sector fortunes and individual differences among REITs are very stark. Picking the right sectors and REITs at different market timings are key in making money and growing your wealth. The silver lining that has emerged is near-zero interest rates. Will this become almost a replay of the post-GFC years from 2008 to 2015 when interest rates remained low and near zero? The US Federal Reserve was only able to increase interest rates by a total of 75 basis points over three raises only in 2017 after 25 basis points increases both in December 2015 and December 2016. Needless to say, REITs thrive when interest rates are expected to remain low for an extended period of time.

LESSON LEARNED

As the COVID-19 Crisis sell-down has shown, REITs are not homogeneous. In fact, the sector fortunes and individual differences among REITs are very stark. Picking the right sectors and REITs at different market timings are key in making money and growing your wealth.

MASTERING THE PSYCHOLOGY OF FEAR

Understanding the psychology of fear is as important as knowing your fundamentals or technical analysis well, going into a crisis market. This has been the hallmark of our Quarterly REITs and Masterclasses that we have been teaching for the past 31 years.

This evolved from my experience navigating the 1987 and 1989 stock market crashes, 1988 Asian Financial Crisis and 2008 Global Financial Crisis. This round of crises have re-affirmed that:

1. Investors are normally ill-prepared to understand and grasp the mathematics of uncertainty, statistical probabilities and Monte Carlo statistical modelling in their risk-return investment projections.[2] It is strange that top schools and colleges teach the mathematics of certainty like trigonometry, differentiation and geometry, but not the mathematics of uncertainty that help investors crystallize their fears and uncertainty. Thus, it is not surprising that investors and traders will over-react, like they did in the four consecutive weeks of sell-downs before the three-day magnificent rebound on Tuesday, 24 March 2020.

2. In a crisis market, investors fear uncertainty, but a crisis is a situation of maximum uncertainty. This creates a sense of loss, desperation and danger. It is in situations like this that investors want firm answers, but it is precisely in such situations where firm answers don't really exist, only the probability bet of certain situations getting worse and the extent where the market has priced that in, that determines profit and loss.

3. Drivers of a REIT's value are its cash flows, growth and risk whereas the determinants of market price are affected by demand and supply factors, including psychological or behavioural factors like momentum, fear and mood in the interim. Prices need not always converge to an intrinsic value, more so during a crisis when momentum, fears and mood drown out the fundamentals and technical elements. Markets are a pricing mechanism, more so in a crisis like COVID-19, as has been demonstrated in previous crises. They may only gravitate towards a weighing mechanism only after prices stabilize.

---

2   "Confabulation is a real problem amongst REIT investors", https://gcpglobalsg.wixsite.com/gcpglobal/post/confabulation-is-a-real-problem-amongst-reit-investors

REITS ARE NOT A GOOD DIVERSIFIER IN TIMES OF CRISIS

Many investors had previously assumed that REITs are a diversifier for their portfolios and fell in love with them for their consistent bond-like dividends. What the COVID-19 Crisis showed was that REITs traded more like other listed equities rather than the more stable real estate that they seek to represent or the stability of bonds. While REITs may have delivered bond-like dividends in the past, the underlying price can swing much more than equities. In fact, for a short time period, losses in REITs surpassed losses in listed equities during a crisis. This same behaviour was borne out during the last Global Financial Crisis.

Additionally, REITs have demonstrated a rising correlation to broad equity markets. According to Thomson Reuters Datastream, the correlation of global REITs to global equites have increased from 0.59 from December 1989 – December 2017 to 0.69 for the period December 2009 – December 2017. For S-REITs, this correlation is also heightened with the number of REITs that are in the FTSE Straits Times Index (STI), which is widely followed by investors as the benchmark of the Singapore market.

When MLT entered the index on 5 December 2019 following MCT on 25 September 2019, it became the fifth REIT in the 30-stock STI, alongside CapitaLand Mall Trust, Ascendas REIT and CapitaLand Commercial Trust. Then, MIT entered the index on 22 June 2020 with a weight of 1.6%. This brought the total number of REITs in the STI to six, with an indicative combined weighting of approximately 12.5%.

What is also interesting is that of the five reserve stocks on the current reserve list, as at September 2020, on the STI Index which now comprise NetLink NBN Trust, Keppel DC REIT, Suntec REIT, Keppel REIT and Frasers Logistics & Commercial Trust, four of them are REITs.

Since REITs are traded more like listed equities, REITs can generate greater risk during severe market stress and volatile market conditions, like what COVID-19 has shown, despite their assumed low-risk profile. Thus, the sharp and smart REIT investor should be cognizant of this fact, be ready to trim his/her portfolio of not-so-good REITs or value traps going into a crisis and be equally adept to catch the strong rebound that REITs have historically been able to stage, based on past crises as well as how this current crisis has shown.

> **LESSON LEARNED**
>
> Since REITs are traded more like listed equities, REITs can generate greater risk during severe market stress and volatile market conditions despite their assumed low-risk profile. Thus, the perspicacious REIT investor should be cognizant of this fact, be ready to trim his/her portfolio of not-so-good REITs or value traps going into a crisis and be equally adept to catch the strong rebound that REITs have historically been able to stage, based on past crises as well as how this current crisis has shown. This is the hallmark of multiplying your wealth in REITs.

NIGHT IS DARKEST BEFORE DAWN

In our weekly Facebook Live sessions beginning Thursday, 19 March 2020 entitled "Navigating the Crisis Market"[3] which have reached more than 30,000 and surpassed 15,000 views, we taught that markets are always the darkest before dawn as it will be hit by one piece of bad news after another.

Five days later, the market subsequently rebounded on Tuesday, 24 March 2020 with the Dow Jones closing up 2,112.98 points or a 11.37% jump, a historic feat. It was the Dow Jones's best day since 15 March 1933.

The bottoms of bear markets always look irrational on hindsight. But in real-time markets like now, fear and greed are the mainstay. As we have taught in our various investment classes, the Smart Investor needs to ferret the gap between a REIT's potential, endure the current volatility which is creating the opportunity to be exploited, and ride the wave.

What I do learn from past crises also, is the fact that markets discount ahead. Why we have been accurate in reading this crisis is my long-held philosophy and attitude in investing and market behaviour: Markets may look bad today, it may be horrible tomorrow or next

3 "Navigating the Current Crisis Market - The Key Psychographics Needed", GCP Global, https://www.facebook.com/watch/live/?v=323200522318452&ref=watch_permalink.

week, but the Smart Investor should recognize that Times Like This Are When Fortunes Are Made.[4]

This has been the tagline all through this crisis in all our various media interviews on Money FM89.3, *Lianhe Zaobao*, *The Straits Times*, *The Business Times*, our weekly Facebook Live sessions, monthly research and monthly online REIT classes throughout this crisis.

CONCLUSION

REITs have evolved into a liquid, institutional investment class. With greater liquidity comes greater volatility, which when harnessed and interpreted appropriately, can lead to great returns. I have been fortunate to be able to do that in my 31 years of direct experience in the financial markets, from being one of Singapore's youngest Head of Research at Nikko Securities (Singapore) Pte Ltd at age 28, to working on Wall Street and then running the Institutional Sales equity desks at several Singapore brokerage firms before retiring in 2009. Thereafter, I have educated and taught REITs to more than 8,000 student investors worldwide in the past 11 years.

As the REIT industry has evolved, unsystematic and company-specific characteristics, rather than broad-brush industry trends and systemic risk, have accounted for outperformance or underperformance of specific REITs. Sector, property-type and many factors cumulatively account for investment returns in different economic environments like the recent COVID-19 crisis.

This is an area of passionate interest that I would like to share in this book as you can build your wealth steadily and consistently with REITs.

---

4   "Fortune Favours the Bold Investor", *The Sunday Times*, 4 November 2009.

Chapter 2

HOW YOU CAN MAKE MILLIONS IN REITS

WHAT IS A REIT?

A real estate investment trust or REIT is a corporate entity that receives revenue through owning and investing in income-producing properties. Thus, as a REIT investor, you actually own a share of the underlying property that the REIT owns. The REIT units are traded on the stock exchange, like stocks or warrants and allow investors ease of purchase or trading.

REITs are collective investment schemes that invest in a portfolio of income generating real estate assets such as shopping malls, offices, hospitals, nursing homes, industrial properties, data centres, hotels and serviced apartments, usually established with a view to generating income for unit holders. Most, if not all REIT laws and legislation try to ensure that REITs derive revenue from stable sources that are not subject to wide fluctuations. A REIT enjoys tax transparency at the REIT level if it pays out at least 90% of its taxable income as distributable income to unit holders.

Many investors buy REITs principally for the attractive dividend yields and good spread to the government bond yield and other competing property investments. Most investors, particularly in Asia, historically gravitate towards investments in a property directly once a certain amount of savings or wealth has been achieved. This is evident from speaking to my multitude of investor students who have attended our classes in the past 31 years where I have been teaching.

As a unit holder of a REIT, investors partake in the benefits and risks of owning a portfolio of property assets that distribute income at regular intervals, mostly quarterly or half-yearly. REITs have regular cash flows as their revenues are derived from rental payments under legally-binding lease contracts with specific rental rates and tenures. Of course, the COVID-19 crisis shattered this long-held notion of Safety of Dividend as addressed in Chapter 1.

ORIGIN OF REITS

REITs were first introduced in the US in 1960 by Congress to allow small investors to have indirect access to large-scale income-producing real estate investments. It started in 1960 with President Eisenhower signing a special tax regulation in which REITs were regarded as profit pass-through vehicles and double taxation was therefore not applicable.

US REITs grew in popularity from the 1960s to 1980, punctuated by bust cycles caused by the stock market crash from 1973 to 1974 which saw interest rates soar to as high as 20% in 1974. In the US, REITs are primarily Equity REITs or Mortgage REITs. The former invests in the ownership position while the latter originate loans that are secured by real estate. Mortgage REITs invest in portfolios of mortgage securities, such as commercial mortgage backed securities (CMBS) and collateralized mortgage obligations (CMOs). Mortgage REITs simply make and hold loans and other bond-like obligations that are backed by real estate. There is another class of REITs known as Hybrid REITs, which as the name suggests, is effectively a combination of equity REITs and mortgage REITs.

Within the two types of REITs, there is further specialization into conventional property type-specific REITs like office, commercial, retail, apartments, shopping centres, industrial, healthcare and hotel REITs. The other specializations are into non-conventional property types like agricultural land, cell tower, data centres, logistics facilities, timber, self-storage and specialized lodgings.

Two other notable developments drove the US REIT market. Tax reform in 1986 allowed REITs to manage and operate real properties directly. In 1993, the restrictions on the investment of pension funds into REITs were removed. These reforms led to a boom in REITs in the 1990s. The legislation changes and reforms were so overwhelming that for the first time, the tables turned as public REITs dominated private equity and private sources of capital in the US commercial real estate market. This turning point came to be known as the "REITs Revolution" in the US REIT market. There are around 153 REITs with a market capitalization of more than US$1.2 trillion.

In Australia, REITs took the form of Listed Property Trusts or LPTs at the beginning in 1971. The Australian REIT market is now very large, well established and sophisticated with approximately 72% of Australian investment grade properties securitized. Commonly known as A-REITs, the market capitalization of listed REITs is approximately valued at more than A$130 billion at end-2019. There are around 40 REITs listed on the Australian Stock Exchange (ASX) which have attracted substantial investments offshore, including significant inflows from Asia and a number of large sovereign wealth funds. In recent years, A-REITs have also expanded internationally into Europe and Asia.

In modern finance, the modern portfolio theory suggests the existence of all assets available for investment. However, real estate assets normally trade less frequently and therefore inclusion in the modern portfolio for valuation purposes is often difficult to replicate and measure. Thus, the availability of REITs which trade on organized securities markets like Wall Street, ASX or the Singapore Stock Exchange is certainly one of the best ways to incorporate real estate assets in modern portfolio theory for analysis and wealth generation.

REITs have become an increasingly popular vehicle in real estate investment globally. There are now almost 40 REIT markets with an estimated market capitalization of more than S$3.5 trillion, up from S$1.1 trillion in 2010. This is a whopping 3x growth in under a decade. The last 15 years have seen a notable increase in the number of countries allowing REITs to flourish in their jurisdictions; more than 18 jurisdictions have introduced REIT or REIT-like legislation since 2005 and this brings the total number of countries with REITs to near 40.

While the US is the most matured REIT market, other established REIT jurisdictions include Austria, France, United Kingdom, Germany and the Netherlands in Europe. In Asia, the more established REIT jurisdictions include Japan, Hong Kong and Singapore. Australia, New Zealand and Canada are the other more established REIT markets.

One common feature of the more established REIT regimes is the relatively higher level of REIT market capitalization/listed real estate market capitalization. Not surprisingly therefore, most of the better-quality assets are owned by REITs in these markets. This characteristic is likely to become more entrenched post-COVID-19 when pandemics, demographics and technology are likely to reshape real estate market dynamics faster.

LESSON LEARNED

Real estate ownership via a REIT structure has taken off sharply, particularly in the past 1.5 decades when market capitalization went up three-fold and more than 18 jurisdictions introduced REIT or REIT-like legislation since 2005 which brings the total number of countries with REITs to near 40. The sagacious REIT investor should take note that invaluable insights gained from trading and investing in REITs in one jurisdiction can be great knowledge in navigating upcoming nascent REIT markets like India and China.

REITS TAKE OFF IN ASIA

REITs first emerged in Asia after the Global Financial Crisis (GFC). Both Singapore and Japan commenced their REIT markets in 2001. Hong Kong, Malaysia, South Korea, Taiwan and Thailand subsequently launched their REIT markets later in the same decade. Japan led the way with the launch of two J-REITs in September 2001. They were the Japan Real Estate Investment Corporation and the Office Building Fund of Japan. Both REITs carried a face value of around US$4,000 and projected dividends of 4-5% and yield spreads of 400 to 500 basis points (bp) over the 10-year bond rate.

In Singapore, the first attempt to launch a REIT actually fell on a flat nose in 2001. It was an initial public offer (IPO) by CapitaLand Group, one of Singapore's largest and leading developers, to list SingMall Property Trust (SPT), which held its various retail properties. I remember clearly as I was then a committee member of the Securities Investors Association of Singapore Executive Council, (SIAS) that helped in the marketing of SPT to retail investors.

Next on the move was Taiwan which launched its first REIT in March 2005. The Fubon No. 1 REIT was listed at a market capitalization of US$186 million. Fubon No. 1 REIT raised TWD5.83 billion (US$194 billion) to acquire two office buildings, an apartment building and a commercial building in Taipei City.

Malaysia also launched its REIT market in August 2005 with the listing of Axis REIT under the new REIT guidelines which had major changes compared to the LPT guidelines which governed some of Malaysia's LPT from 1989. Axis REIT IPO was quickly followed by YTL REIT which owned prime assets in Kuala Lumpur like the JW Marriott Hotel, Starhill Shopping Centre and Lot 10 Shopping Centre.

2005 ended with a major REIT development. The Hong Kong Housing Authority tried to securitize some of its suburban shopping centres and car parks through Link REIT. After a shareholder protest which initially led to the IPO being withdrawn, Link REIT which was offered at a dividend yield of 6% or a yield spread of approximately 335 bp, finally got off the starting block in November 2005. Link REIT was a widely-watched IPO as not only was it the first HK-REIT, it was also the largest REIT IPO in the world at a market capitalization of US$2.6 billion.

Moreover, it was quickly followed by two other REIT listings, namely GZI REIT and Prosperity, both of which were listed in December 2005.

REITS TAKE OFF IN SINGAPORE

When SingMall Property Trust (SPT) was first offered at a 5.75% yield as Singapore's first REIT IPO, it failed in November 2001. The intended offer size then was $740 million of which $530 million or

71.6% were to be offered to the public and institutional investors for the IPO priced at $1.

At 5.75%, SPT had a yield spread of only 281 basis points (lower than the two J-REITs launched earlier in 2001) at a time when the 10-year government bond yield was 2.89% and fixed deposit rates from the major banks hovered between 1.75–1.9%. The launch was poorly received with low subscription rates and led to the IPO being withdrawn.

In my view, the IPO failed due to a combination of valuation and poor market timing. The yield offered was not high enough and the discount to its NAV was not deep enough to sway investors to Singapore's first-ever REIT IPO. Furthermore, issues on the valuation of the three assets for the initial REIT portfolio arose which heightened investors' fears on the downside risk of SPT valuation. Moreover, REITs were new to Singapore investors and prospects for the retail market were poor as the economy was just recovering from the two-year slump caused by the Asian Financial Crisis from 1997 to 1998.

SPT, renamed CapitaMall Trust, was subsequently floated on 17 July 2002. This time, the yield was a more persuasive 7.06%, offering a good spread of close to 480 basis points to the 10-year bond yield at an offer price of $0.96. And the market took it well – it was more than five times oversubscribed.

Next to list was Ascendas REIT in November 2002. Its IPO was also well-subscribed by more than five times. Next to follow was Fortune REIT, the first cross-border REIT in Asia. CapitaCommercial Trust (CCT), now known as Capital Commercial Trust and Suntec subsequently followed, listing in 2004. CCT's listing was notable as it was spun out of its parent, CapitaLand, as the latter's shareholders received 1 CCT share for every 5 held as part of a capital reduction exercise.

	IPO DATE	IPO PRICE	DPU till 2019	DPU 1Q2020	Total DPU	Price 30/06/2020	% Change
CapitaMall Trust	17/07/2002	$0.96	$1.7892	$ 0.0085	$1.7977	$1.9600	104.17%

CMT's returns since IPO

Over the years, CapitaMall Trust, now known as CapitaLand Mall Trust, has done spectacularly well. Investors who bought the IPO at $0.96 would have enjoyed a capital gain of more than 104.17% based on the closing price of $1.96 as at 30 June 2020. Taking into account the dividends earned of $1.7977 over the past seventeen years, the total gain would have been $2.7977 or a total return of 291.43%. This works out to a Compound Annual Growth Return (CAGR) of 6.49%, a good example of how the smart and sharp REIT investor can make millions investing in the right REIT at IPO.

	Total Return		CAGR	
	$	%	Total	%
CapitaMall Trust	$2.7977	291.43%	2.7977	6.49%

CMT's CAGR since IPO

LESSON LEARNED

REIT IPOs can fail if valuations are not sufficiently attractive. Whilst valuation metrics like dividend yield and discount to NAV can vary with the economic cycle and stage of the property market, proper execution of a successful REIT IPO needs an astute reading and understanding of market timing and investors' appetite.

One of the changes that fuelled the appetite for S-REITs was the change in granting tax transparency in December 2002. The rule was relaxed to not less than 90% of income distribution requirement, from 100%. The tax transparency status was also extended to include Singapore permanent residents who are tax residents in the republic and other non-corporate Singapore registered entities.

To sustain the growth of the S-REIT market, the Singapore government introduced a series of changes to the regulatory framework in 2005. It announced the waiver of stamp duties for properties acquired by REITs over a period of five years. This was the government's recognition that REITs actually help enlarge and deepen the country's capital markets and help grow the local fund management industry, an area that was competing closely with Hong Kong.

Other areas of improvement involved incorporating more flexibility in undertaking international expansion, aligning investors' interest with that of the REIT managers and the possibility of raising the gearing ratio of REITs from the then 35% to 60%, subject to a credit-rating.

All the above changes paved the way for a record listing of nine REITs in Singapore in 2006 and three in 2007 just before the GFC set in. With the GFC in full rage in 2008 and 2009, there were no new listings in Singapore till the dust settled in 2010 when three new listings, namely Cache Logistics, now renamed as ARA Logos Logistics Trust, Mapletree Industrial Trust and Sabana REIT debuted.

The benchmark FTSE ST Real Estate Index was launched in 2008. It comprised the FTSE Real Estate Investment & Service Index and FTSE ST Real Estate Investment Trust (FTSE REIT) Index. The latter has been widely used as a barometer of S-REITs performance thereafter.

REITS VS PROPERTY INVESTMENT

By being public, REITs are accessible to investors of all types – pension funds, institutional funds, family offices, high net worth investors and individuals. The beauty is that the job of purchasing, managing or directly financing the properties is left to the REIT manager who performs or appoints professionals for these various tasks.

There are certainly advantages to owning a property outright, but the comparative benefits of REITs are now becoming more evident than the former. I expect this trend to change steadily and consistently as investors get a better understanding about the outperformance of REITs verses not just physical property, but other asset classes.

Refer to Chapter 3 on the liquidity advantage of REITs vs other asset classes.

A key attraction of REITs for investors has been their relative high yield as compared to equities and bonds. This is due to the Monetary Authority of Singapore (MAS) regulation that requires all

REITs to pay out at least 90% of their profits as dividends. Over the course of the development of the REIT industry in Singapore since 2002, dividend yields have ranged from 5.5% to 11.5% during 2002 to 2007, 7.5% to 18% during the Global Financial Crisis (GFC) of 2008 to 2009, 6% to 9.5% from 2011 to 2013 and 4.5% to 11.5% from 2014 to 2019.

The MAS REIT regulations follow closely the Real Estate Investment Trust Act of 1960 in America that paved the way for the development of the REIT industry. Unique to REITs, is their tax status – they pay no corporate tax as long as they distribute at least 90% of their income as dividends, among other specific criteria.

Actually, it is not much difficult to understand why REITs can actually outperform most other asset classes. The steady and regular dividends that REITs pay, utilizing the power of compounding, is the key for such an outperformance, while avoiding the value traps.

REITS TOTAL RETURNS SINCE THE INCEPTION OF THE REIT SECTOR

I was first attracted to REITs in a big way after I retired in 2009 in my early 40s[1] to travel and live around the world. As the US REIT market is the oldest REIT market in the world, it was noteworthy that US equity REITs only suffered losses in 8 out of the 40 years when I studied the first available data from 1971 to 2010. Intuitively, the odds are indeed very favourable mathematically. In fact, there were only three occasions when US REITs suffered back-to-back year-on-year declines in the same period. That to me is a good indication of how much you can lose.

US Equity REITs		
Year	No. of REITs	Total Return
1973	20	-15.50%
1974	19	-21.40%
1987	53	-3.60%
1990	58	-15.40%
1998	173	-17.50%

---

1   "Millionaire with heart of Gold", *The Sunday Times*, 6 December 2009.

1999	167	-4.60%
2007	118	-15.70%
2008	113	-37.70%

US equity REIT performance from 1970 to 2010 registered only 8 losses out of the past 40 years.
Source – National Association of Real Estate Investment Trusts, NAREIT

Total returns of US REITs have since outpaced equities as measured by the Dow Jones and Standard & Poor's 500 Index (S&P 500) over long investment periods. For instance, US REITs had an annualized return of 16.7% from 1975 to 2006, a 30-year period. Data from NAREIT showed that total returns for US REITs averaged 12.87% per year from 31 December 1978 to 31 March 2016, as compared to just 11.64% per year for stocks. Compared with the S&P 500 which registered a return of 12.2%, US REITs beat the S&P 500 with its return of 14.1% from 1975 to 2014, a 40-year period. Essentially, US REITs have outperformed both bonds and equities for a substantial period of time in the past 60 years.

My investment and teachings in REITs are largely driven to earn a risk-adjusted return similar to or exceeding common stock, but with less variability and volatility.

My 31-year experience in the investment field, first as Head of Research, working on Wall Street and then running the institutional sales desks at various financial institutions, has helped me tremendously in knowing when to bet on REITs in a big way.[2]

S-REITS RETURNS IN THE PREVIOUS DECADE

There were 21 REITs listed from 2002 to 2010. Saizen REIT was subsequently taken over and delisted on 2012.

Eleven out of the 20 REITs delivered compounded annual growth returns (CAGR) of more than 8% to the REIT investor. This means that you would have doubled your investment capital every 8.5 years if you had invested in these 11 REITs since their respective Initial Public Offer (IPO). These are certainly very good odds on a mathematical basis.

---

2   "Bet big in times of crisis: GCP Global's Gabriel Yap," *The Business Times*, 10 April 2017.

REITS PERFORMANCE SINCE IPO	IPO DATE	IPO PRICE	Total DPU ($)	Price 31/12/2019	% Change	Total Return $	%	CAGR Total ($)	%
CapitaMall Trust	Jul-02	$0.960	1.7892	$2.460	256.25%	3.2892	342.63%	4.2492	9.14%
Ascendas REIT	Nov-02	$0.880	2.3190	$2.970	337.50%	4.4090	501.02%	5.2890	11.13%
Capital Commercial	May04	$1.00	1.1880	$2.010	201.00%	2.1980	219.80%	3.1980	8.06%
Suntec REIT	Dec-04	$1.000	1.3840	$1.840	184.00%	2.2240	222.40%	3.2240	8.12%
Mapletree Logistics Trust	Jul-05	$0.680	1.0400	$1.740	255.88%	2.1000	308.83%	2.7800	10.58%
Starhill Global REIT	Sep-05	$0.980	0.6983	$0.725	73.98%	0.4433	45.23%	1.4233	2.70%
Ascott REIT	Mar 06	$0.680	1.0135	$1.330	195.59%	1.6635	244.63%	2.3435	9.99%
Frasers Comm Trust	Mar 06	$1.000	0.9180	$1.660	166.00%	1.5780	157.80%	2.5780	7.56%
Keppel REIT	Apr-06	$1.040	0.8676	$1.230	118.27%	1.0576	101.69%	2.0976	5.54%
Frasers Centrepoint Trust	Jul-06	$1.030	1.3372	$2.880	279.61%	3.1872	309.44%	4.2172	11.45%
CDL HT	Jul-06	$0.830	1.3113	$1.620	195.18%	2.1013	253.17%	2.9313	10.19%
Cambridge REIT	Jul-06	$0.680	0.6461	$0.535	78.68%	0.5011	73.68%	1.1811	4.34%
Capital Retail China	Dec-06	$1.130	1.1632	$1.590	140.71%	1.6232	143.65%	2.7532	7.09%
First REIT	Dec-06	$0.710	1.0135	$1.030	145.07%	1.3335	187.82%	2.0435	8.47%

SREIT IPOs 2002 to 2006 and their total returns till end-2019

The top five REITs delivered CAGR of between 10.58% to 16.13% return or an average of 12.54%. This means that if you had the ability and skill to pick the top five performing REITs (I am a top-20 shareholder of Frasers Centrepoint Trust since IPO and am a shareholder of Mapletree Industrial Trust, Ascendas REIT and Mapletree Logistics Trust) since their IPO, you would have been able to double your investment capital approximately every six years – that's the power of dividend compounding and the ability to pick out the winners in REITs.

Using Frasers Centrepoint Trust as an illustration since I have been a top-20 shareholder for FCT since IPO, 1 million units of FCT costing a total of $1.03 million at IPO would have yielded you total dividends of $1.33 million in the past 13 years till end-2019. The same 1 million units of FCT bought at $1.03 is worth $2.88 million at end-2019. Thus, the total gain is $3.18 million! And as long as you remain as its shareholder, you will continue to reap dividends every quarter. FCT's CAGR worked out to 11.45% per annum for the past 13 years. You will double your investment capital in FCT every 6.5 years approximately if this trend continues.

Only two REITs, namely Lippo Malls and Sabana REIT yielded negative CAGR returns. Thus, a $1 million investment in either Lippo Malls or Sabana REIT at IPO would have yielded negative returns whereas the same $1 million invested in any of the top five REITs would have yielded a difference of more than $3 million from their respective IPOs till 2019. Both Lippo Malls and Sabana REIT prices remained below half their IPO price as at June 2020. The stark difference in wealth clearly exemplifies that when it comes to REITs, having and holding the right REITs that can deliver multiple year returns via dividends and capital gain is the greatest determinant.

We have seen bad apples like MacarthurCook Industrial REIT and Allco REIT running into trouble during the last Global Financial Crisis of 2007 to 2009; both have been taken over and are presently known as AIMS AMP REIT and Frasers Commercial Trust, respectively.

Excluding these bad apples, it is clear that the historical performance of S-REITs has been remarkable and should inch up

REITS PERFORMANCE	IPO	IPO	Total	Price	%	Total Return		CAGR	
SINCE IPO	DATE	PRICE	DPU ($)	31/12/2019	Change	$	%	Total ($)	%
AIMS AMP REIT	Apr07	$1.200	1.0750	$1.430	119.17%	1.3050	108.75%	2.5050	6.33%
Parkway Life	Aug07	$1.280	1.3298	$3.320	259.38%	3.3698	263.27%	4.6498	11.35%
Lippo Malls Trust	Nov07	$0.800	0.4219	$0.225	28.13%	-0.1531	-19.14%	0.6469	-1.75%
Cache Logistics	Apr10	$0.880	0.7376	$0.715	81.25%	0.5726	65.07%	1.4526	5.73%
Mapletree Industrial Trust	Oct10	$0.930	0.9717	$2.600	279.57%	2.6417	284.05%	3.5717	16.13%
Sabana REIT	Nov10	$1.050	0.5641	$0.460	43.81%	-0.0259	-2.47%	1.0241	-0.28%

S-REIT IPOs 2007 to 2010 and their Total Returns till end-2019

a higher proportion in one's investment portfolio if you are looking to double or triple your wealth on a steady and consistent basis. Of course, historical performance may not repeat itself in the same manner in the future, but if it does, the sharp and smart REIT investor should be prepared to take advantage of this.

Clearly, it exemplifies what we have been teaching all these years –

LESSON LEARNED

1. S-REITs have provided investors with long term sustainable total returns.
2. On a risk-adjusted basis, S-REITs have outperformed both bonds and equities.
3. But to be able to achieve that, it is imperative for the investor to be able to pick the right REITs for your portfolio to achieve consistent and steady returns over the years and decades.
4. Side-stepping bad apples is part and parcel of REIT investing. The smart and sharp REIT investor needs to understand when to ditch these apples before they turn bad or to recognize conditions that will make these apples turn bad subsequently.

S-REITS 10-YEAR ANNUALIZED TOTAL RETURNS

An annualized total return is defined as the geometric average amount of money earned by an investment each year, over a given time period. An annualized total return provides a snapshot of an investment's performance, but does not give any indication of its volatility or price fluctuations.

In the local context, the latest figures on 10-Year Annualized Total Returns (ATR) from SGX and Bloomberg, as at November 2019, are quite revealing in that –

1.   Fourteen out of the 18 REITs would have given you an ATR of near 10% or more. If a smart investor had avoided the market corrections in 2011, 2013, 2015 and 2018, the ATRs would be even higher.

2.   It continued to reinforce and exemplify the trends in total returns that REITs had been able to deliver in the previous decade: S-REITs are able to deliver sustainable and gradual total returns.

3. The top three REITs, namely Frasers Commercial Trust achieved ATR of 16.6%, Mapletree Logistics Trust at 16.5% and Parkway Life at 15.9%. Like the top five performing REITs of the previous decade, a REIT investor would have been able to double their investment capital every eight years if they know how to pick the correct winners.

4. Thus, it reinforces what we have been teaching in our REITs Quarterly and Master classes in the past decade – market timing for REITs is important for superior performances and having and holding the right REITs in your REIT portfolio will determine your long-term wealth.

S-REITS RETURNS IN THE PAST DECADE

The FTSE ST REIT Index has delivered five-year total returns of 38% from 2013 to 2018. Bear in mind that this five-year period includes two REIT corrections of 22.5% during the Taper Tantrum and the vicious 15.83% sell-off in 2015.

The FTSE ST REIT Index then close up 15.53% in 2019 and is down only 11.53% in 1H2020 despite going through the torturous and painful COVID-19 pandemic sell-off which many have compared to the crisis of the GFC in 2008 and the Great Depression of 1929 at the height of the sell-off on 23 March 2020. Even as this book goes into print, many prognosticators are still calling for the bottom of 23 March 2020 to be re-tested.

However, not many REITs that had their IPO in the past decade have done well.

REITS WITH IPO IN PAST DECADE	IPO Date	IPO Price	30-Jun-20	Price Change	% Change
Mapletree Commercial	27th Apr 2011	$0.88	$1.930	$1.050	119.32%
Ascendas Hospitality Trust	26th Jul 2012	$0.88		MERGED	
Far East Hospitality Trust	24th Aug 2012	$0.93	$0.495	($0.435)	-46.77%
Mapletree Greater China	7th Mar 2013	$0.92	$0.925	$0.005	0.54%

Croesus Retail Trust	10th May 2013	$0.93		PRIVATISED	
SPH REIT	24th Jul 2013	$0.90	$0.875	($0.025)	-2.78%
OUE Hospitality Trust	25th Jul 2013	$0.88		MERGED	
Soilbuild Business Space REIT	16th Aug 2013	$0.78	$0.390	($0.390)	-50.00%
Viva Industrial Trust	4th Nov 2013	$0.78		MERGED	

REIT IPOs, 2011 to 2013

Since 2011 till mid-2020, there have been 25 REIT IPOs on the SGX.

Only five of the IPOs have generated positive capital gains out of the 25. Excluding the likes of Ascendas India Trust, OUE Hospitality Trust and Viva Trust, all of which have been merged with another REIT and Croesus Retail Trust was privatized. The remaining 16 REITs have generated negative capital returns for the REIT investor. The means that almost four out of every five REITs that listed since 2011 till mid-2020 registered negative capital returns. This can be quite shocking for some REIT investors, but there are a few reasons behind this phenomenon which we have forewarned the student investors in our REITs classes.

REITS WITH IPO IN PAST DECADE	IPO Date	IPO Price	30-Jun-20	Price Change	% Change
OUE Commercial Trust	27th Jan 2014	$0.80	$0.380	($0.420)	-52.50%
Frasers Hospitality Trust	16th Jul 2014	$0.88	$0.465	($0.415)	-47.16%
IREIT	13th Aug 2014	$0.88	$0.725	($0.155)	-17.61%
Keppel DC REIT	12th Dec 2014	$0.93	$2.550	$1.620	174.19%
BHG Retail REIT	11th Dec 2015	$0.80	$0.585	($0.215)	-26.88%
Manulife REIT	12th May 2016	$0.83	$0.755	($0.075)	-9.04%

| Frasers Logistics & Comm | 21st Jun 2016 | $0.89 | $1.190 | $0.300 | 33.71% |
| EC World REIT | 26th Jul 2016 | $0.81 | $0.690 | ($0.120) | -14.81% |

REIT IPOs, 2014 to 2016

One phenomenon that stands out is that since 2011, only 8 out of the 25 REITs that came up for IPO, have the majority of their assets in Singapore. The rest of the 17 REITs were listed with most of their assets outside Singapore. In fact, 19 out of the 43 S-REITs have real estate portfolios entirely composed of overseas properties as at June 2020.

REITS WITH IPO IN PAST DECADE	IPO Date	IPO Price	30-Jun-20	Price Change	% Change
Keppel KBS REIT, US$	9th Nov 2017	$0.88	$0.700	($0.180)	-20.45%
Cromwell REIT, Euro	30th Nov 2017	$0.55	$0.420	($0.130)	-23.64%
Sasseur REIT	29th Mar 2018	$0.80	$0.740	($0.060)	-7.50%
ARA US Hospitality Trust	9th May 2019	$0.88	$0.400	($0.480)	-54.55%
Eagle Hospitality Trust	24th May 2019	$0.78	$0.137	($0.643)	-82.44%
Prime US REIT	19th Jul 2019	$0.88	$0.780	($0.100)	-11.36%
Lendlease Commercial REIT	2nd Oct 2019	$0.88	$0.680	($0.200)	-22.73%
Elite Commercial REIT	6th Feb 2020	$0.68	$0.700	$0.020	2.94%
United Hampshire	11th Mar 2020	$0.80	$0.590	($0.210)	-26.25%

REIT IPOs, 2017 to 2020.

Understandably, due to limited investible local assets, most REITs that IPO since 2011 are predominantly those with assets overseas and even local REITs have been increasingly looking abroad for growth via acquisitions. However, growth via overseas acquisitions does not equate to growth in REIT prices for REIT holders as overseas acquisitions should be analysed with greater scrutiny due to limited information and sometimes, a lack of independent grounds for verification of certain trends and facts in relation to reversionary rentals, occupancies and tenants' veracity of the REIT's IPO portfolio or acquired properties post-IPO.

For instance, most analysts assess REIT acquisitions based on the presentation materials dished out by the REITs, which naturally dispense positive information to justify their acquisitions. The smart investor should always question if some of the information dished out to justify the acquisitions are indeed verifiable to justify the price paid. This becomes a more difficult process if the properties are located in countries that are less well-known to the investor or it becomes difficult to independently verify some of other key metrics underlying the REIT's asset portfolio at IPO or future acquisitions.

Moreover, REITs with foreign assets are of higher risk for REIT investors, as detailed in Chapter 6 of this book. For instance, investors were treated to a scare in 2018 over the tax transparency of REITs with US assets which sent the share prices of Manulife and Keppel KBS REIT, now known as Keppel Oak Pacific REIT, down more than 20% in a matter of days.

In analysing the performance of the 26 S-REITs that listed in the past decade based on the 30 June 2020 closing prices, it may come as a shock to many investors that –

1. Only 5 out of 22 (excluding those that were privatized or merged since) have posted capital gains compared to their IPO prices. The great thing is that some of the gains posted by the five winners are really outsized gains like Mapletree Commercial Trust's 119.32% and Keppel DC REIT's 174.19%.

2. Six out of the 17 losers registered losses of more than 40% as compared to their respective IPO prices. The worst losers were Eagle Hospitality Trust at 88.44% (currently suspended as this book goes to print), ARA US Hospitality Trust at 54.55% and OUE Commercial Trust at 52.5%.

3. Almost all REITs with 100% or near-100% overseas assets suffered losses. The exceptions were Frasers Logistics &

Commercial Trust and Elite Commercial REIT. And even the gains are fairly mixed. While Frasers Logistics posted a handsome 33.71% gain, Elite Commercial REIT only managed a 2 cents or 2.94% gain.

The average performance of the 22 REITs (after excluding the four that either merged or were privatized) that listed in the past decade was -8.44%. So, what are the realities and opportunities for REIT investors looking to invest into REITs with 100% or near-100% of their assets outside Singapore?

We have always taught that –

1.   REIT buyers should always assess if the risk at IPO is commensurate with the expected returns that they are promising. Media hype and the self-interest of IPO aspirants, underwriters and bankers should be understood and discounted by the smart REIT investor.

2.   REIT investors should always be cognizant of potential shortcomings in the underwriting process of a REIT IPO. REIT Sponsors almost always try to maximize the price they can get from the IPO market. While every conceivable risk and event is highlighted in IPO prospectuses, few investors have the time, let alone the knowledge to read through the 1,000+ pages in a REIT IPO prospectus. For instance, Eagle Hospitality Trust, which ran into trouble shortly after its IPO, has 890 pages in its IPO prospectus. The thickest IPO prospectus goes to Cromwell European REIT with 1,066 pages.

3.   Not all REITs fall into the same basket. Although REITs in general have outperformed the capital markets, it is imperative for the investor to be able to pick the right REITs[3] for your portfolio for consistent and steady returns over the years and decades.

Understandably, from a REIT perspective, expanding into multiple countries provides growth opportunities, economies of scale and diversification. For instance, Mapletree North Asia Commercial Trust,

---

3   "The Great Market Divide", *The Sunday Times*, 31 May 2009.

formerly known as Mapletree Greater China, acquired six freehold office properties in Tokyo, Chiba and Yokohama for a total acquisition cost of about JPY63,304 million (US$572 million) in January 2018. One of the key considerations was the freehold tenure of the Japanese portfolio which balanced out the leasehold assets in China and Hong Kong.

LESSON LEARNED

Almost four out of every five S-REITs that listed since 2011 till mid-2020 have registered negative capital returns. The perspicacious REIT investor should recognize that not all REITs fall into the same basket. Although REITs in general have outperformed the capital markets, it is imperative for the investor to be able to pick the right REITs for your portfolio for consistent and steady returns over the years and decades, especially when the future development of S-REITs is slanted towards one with more or predominantly foreign assets.

Chapter 3

WHY YOU SHOULD HAVE REITS IN YOUR INVESTMENT PORTFOLIO

Many investors buy REITs principally for the attractive dividend yields and good spread to the government bonds yields and other competing property investments. REITs have unique characteristics that make them attractive to both income and growth investors. REITs trade like stocks and can fluctuate in prices, but they also pay out a large part of their income in the form of dividends. Actually, there are more compelling reasons to include REITs as part of a well-balanced investment portfolio.

Most investors, particularly in Asia, historically gravitate towards direct investments in property once a certain amount of savings or wealth has been achieved. This is evident from speaking to my multitude of investor students who have attended our classes in the past 31 years where I have been teaching. As stocks, bonds and REITs react to the same economic changes differently and in varying degrees, combining these assets together in an investment portfolio helps to produce an offsetting risk-and-return trade-off. This makes REITs a good addition for investors looking to build diversified portfolios.

There are certainly advantages to owning a property outright, but the comparative benefits of REITs are now becoming more evident than the former. I expect this trend to change steadily and consistently as investors get a better understanding about the outperformance of REITs versus not just physical property, but other asset classes as well.

Actually, it is not difficult to understand why REITs can actually outperform most other asset classes. The steady and regular dividends that REITs pay, utilizing the power of compounding, is the key to such an outperformance.

DIVIDENDS

Steady dividend income is one of the primary reasons for investment in REITs. REITs have a fairly stable income stream from rental collections paid by tenants bound by their lease agreements over a certain period of time. Hence, the regular and stable nature of such cash dividend income is highly rated. This dividend yield is even more attractive when compared to other asset classes like equities, bonds, real estate and the Central Provident Fund (CPF) rate.

Chapter 4 discusses the characteristics of REIT dividends and an analysis of dividend yield. This helps the investor to judge the sustainability of a REIT's dividends, a key topic brought to the forefront of most investors' concern during the COVID-19 Pandemic when REIT rentals across most sectors were suspended in many countries.

REITs have a reasonably consistent payout ratio at an index level which makes the dividend yield an excellent proxy of value. When yields are high, it is generally an indication of good value and when yields are low, it is an indication that REITs are getting more expensive. This has resulted in the use of the Yield Spread as a valuation benchmark.

Yield Spread = Dividend Yield from REITs –
10-year Government Bond Yield

The Yield Spread has varied depending on different
interest rate environment.

REITs are an attractive investment for people looking for current income, provided the REIT has a conservatively leveraged balance sheet, good asset quality, managed by a good REIT manager and supported by a good sponsor. When a REIT possesses these qualities, it generally can grow its Distribution Per Unit (DPU) on a consistent and sustainable basis. These are the kind of REITs that investors should look for.

> **LESSON LEARNED**
>
> Steady dividend income is one of the primary reasons for investment in REITs. REITs have a fairly stable income stream from rental collections paid by tenants bound by their lease agreements over a certain period of time. For the risk-adverse investor, investing in REITs that can grow their DPU on a consistent and steady basis without taking on undue risk is certainly one of the best ways of growing wealth.

TOTAL RETURNS

Total Returns = Sum of DPU received + Capital Gain (or Loss)

As REITs' DPU are stable and predictable, they have helped boost Total Returns of REITs to exceed that of equities, bonds and real estate for an extended period of time in many jurisdictions with REITs markets, as detailed in Chapter 2. This has endeared many funds, institutional monies, family offices and individual investors to this asset class.

We have detailed in Chapter 2 that the diligent and sharp REIT investor can make millions if you invest in the right REITs as they had delivered compounded annual growth returns (CAGR) of more than 8% to the REIT investor. This means that you would have doubled your investment capital every 8.5 years if you had invested in these REITs since their respective Initial Public Offer (IPO).

LIQUIDITY

Publicly traded REITs offer investors the eclectic ability to add real estate returns to their investment portfolio without incurring illiquidity risk that is embedded in direct real estate investments. This is so because REITs that are publicly traded on stock exchanges can be bought and sold in any volumes and minimal bid/ask spread differences. This is unlike direct real estate investment deals which normally take a few months, if not years to consummate a deal, especially when the property market is unfavourable or when interest rates are not favourable. REITs therefore allow investors to undertake real estate investments in a liquid and easy manner.

As liquid investments with instantaneous pricing, REITs allow investors the flexibility to quickly adjust their exposure to different asset classes and within the real estate asset class, with ease and at a low cost.

Shares of S-REITs are bought and sold on the Singapore Exchange (SGX) daily. There are 43 REITs with a combined market capitalization of close to $100 billion as at June 2020 on the SGX. The trading volume of REITs as a percentage of total traded stocks on the SGX has steadily risen over the decades and now constitutes about 30% of daily trading volumes. S-REITs now comprise about 15% of the SGX market capitalization. In fact, S-REITs market capitalization has grown at a CAGR of 15% over the past decade. Other than institutional and individual investors, there are many REIT mutual funds and Exchange Traded Funds (EFTs) that invest and trade in REITs.

GCP Management Holdings investor students love REITs for their liquidity, especially when you know how to trade them profitably.

LESSON LEARNED

As liquid investments with instantaneous pricing, REITs allow investors to adjust the risk-return profile of their investment portfolios quickly. It offers flexibility to investors to quickly adjust their exposure to different asset classes and within the real estate asset class, with ease and at a low cost. Also, with the correct knowledge, investors can trade profitably in REITs.

PORTFOLIO DIVERSIFICATION

Investors who diversify their investment portfolios have historically achieved higher rates of returns because diversification reduces portfolio volatility and mitigates losses from any one asset class. While a diversified portfolio may not deliver skyscraper returns, history has shown that slow and steady wins the race. The logic is that gains from some investments will offset the losses sustained by other investments, thereby improving the bottom line while reducing overall portfolio risk.

REITs generally own multiple property portfolios in a certain sector/geography or across sectors or geographies. They come with diversified tenant pool, thereby reducing the risks of reliance on a single property or tenant as compared to owning real estate directly. This provides investors with the opportunity to invest in a diversified pool of real estate assets or portfolios for a modest sum of capital.

REITs have proven to be effective portfolio diversification tools in multiple studies, using different combination of techniques, data sources, time periods and across different geographical regions. These studies have revealed that REITs can increase portfolio returns without increasing portfolio risk or maintain returns while lowering overall portfolio risks.

The reason for this is easy to understand as investing in real estate through REITs has its own unique drivers and cycles which can be distinct or differ in magnitude from equities, bonds and direct real estate investment.

Many studies have shown that the outperformance of REITs can be largely attributed to the resilience and consistency of the DPU payout of REITs, but an equally important factor is the low correlation that REITs have with equities, bonds and direct real estate investment. For instance, equities are driven by the business cycle, which is the rise and fall of economic activities. When the business cycle is expanding, market returns are good. However, when it contracts and falls into a recession, equities can suffer losses. REITs may follow a completely different real estate cycle which runs counter to the business cycle or differ in length of each up or down cycle. This provides effective diversification.

Generally, a correlation of +1 means a high level of linkage in price movements in the same direction while a correlation of -1 means a high level of linkage in price movements in the opposite direction. REITs in most jurisdictions, generally have a correlation of less than 0.8 over different periods of times with the different asset classes. In other words, REIT returns have tended to go up while returns of other asset classes have lagged, and vice versa, smoothing a diversified portfolio's overall volatility.

REITs tend to have a lower-than-average correlation with other asset classes; although they are affected by broader market trends, their performances can be expected to deviate from the major market indices of bonds or equities. This performance makes them a powerful hedging vehicle without taking on additional risk.

Increasingly, S-REITs are offering investors diversification exposure beyond Singapore as they undertake yield-accretive acquisitions of properties from China to the US and from Seoul to Seattle. In fact, close to 80% of S-REITs presently own properties outside Singapore which provides a natural geographical diversification for S-REIT investors. This also means that the number of S-REITs with 100% Singapore-based assets are now confined to just five, namely, CapitaLand Mall Trust, Frasers Centrepoint Trust, Mapletree Commercial Trust, Far East Hospitality Trust and ESR-REIT.

Our Singapore REITs Symposium 2018 where investors are shown how REITs can effectively diversify one's investment portfolio.

LESSON LEARNED

REITs have proven to be effective portfolio diversification tools in multiple studies using different combinations of techniques, data sources, time periods and across different geographical regions. REITs have been shown to increase portfolio returns without increasing portfolio risk or have been able to maintain returns while lowering overall portfolio risks.

INFLATION HEDGE

Over different cycles, REITs have proven to be able to increase their rental rates in line with inflation, thereby providing an effective inflation hedge, unlike bonds. Over the long term, REITs do become more correlated with property returns and offer more inflation hedging capabilities, but not all REIT sectors offer the same level of inflation hedge due to the characteristics of the underlying leases. In fact, the COVID-19 Pandemic brought to the attention of REIT investors once again that due to the strong correlation of equities and REITs during a crisis sell-down, REITs were not as strong an inflation hedge as previously thought, especially in times of crisis.

REITs have delivered total returns that exceeded the Financial

Times Straits Times Index (FTSE STI) as elaborated in Chapter 2. In addition, dividends generally increase faster than inflation, using the Consumer Price Index as a benchmark.

Investors have favoured REITs that are able to structure their leases in such a way where increases in operating costs are passed along to the tenant. For example, investors would prefer REIT landlords to be able to charge tenants for costs like utilities, insurance, taxes. This can be done in a few ways –

1. Have annual rental rate increase clauses in the leases, as many data centre and industrial REITs do.
2. Have triple-net leases whereby the tenant pays for all the operating costs like in the case of many of Keppel DC REIT leases in the data centre sector.

The result is that REITs can generate inflation-adjusted earnings, which make their REIT price attractive even in times of inflation.

Shorter-term leases and inflation-linked leases are better inflation hedges because the landlord can reprice rental rates more frequently. This is advantageous when inflation accelerates and the landlord can raise rentals to market rates faster. This of course is more prevalent in sectors like hospitality, hotels, serviced apartments, residential apartments and shopping malls. Contrast this with REITs with longer-term leases like healthcare, triple-net leases and data centres.

LESSON LEARNED

The inclusion of annual rental rate increase clauses or triple-net leases whereby the tenant pays for all the operating costs, like in the case of many leases in the data centre and industrial sector have enabled REITs to generate inflation-adjusted earnings. This makes their REIT price attractive even in times of inflation.

A GOOD DIVERSIFIER OF WEALTH

REITs are a good diversification tool. Much research has proven that investing in REITs helps lower overall portfolio risk and increases returns on a portfolio of equities, bonds, foreign currencies, commodities and real estate. Long-term total returns from REITs tend to be similar to those of blue-chip stocks and higher than the returns from AAA-rated bonds.

REITs are popular with investors who view stocks as too volatile, bonds as not giving enough yield, especially during times of very low interest rates and less cumbersome to own when compared to direct real estate. REITs complement other types of investments by offering a defensive position during volatile market conditions. Because of the strong dividend income that REITs provide, they are an important investment both for passive income investors as well as retirees who require a continuing income stream to meet daily living expenses. This phenomenon has been well played out from the developed REIT markets like the US, Australia, Japan, Singapore and Hong Kong to new REIT jurisdictions like India and Philippines and to aspirants like China.

Thus, an allocation to REITs can reduce an investment portfolio's overall volatility while simultaneously increasing its yield. Another advantage of REITs over bonds is that unlike bonds which are redeemed at par on maturity, REITs have the potential for long term capital appreciation. Of course, the sharp and smart REIT investor should avoid those REITs that have the likelihood of delivering negative capital returns as elaborated upon at length in Chapter 2. REITs are also available in a diversified, liquid, low-cost investment product like the various REIT index funds and ETFs if the REIT investor choses to pick a basket of REITs instead of picking individual REITs for their portfolio.

In fact, studies have shown that from 1975 through 2006 in the US, over a 30-year period, a portfolio divided 50/50 between stocks and REITs would have returned 15.2% as compared to 13.5% if invested in the S&P 500 alone. The frosting on the cake – this stellar result was achieved with 12% lower risk!

Past studies have attempted to determine whether the addition of REITs to a diversified common stock portfolio would enhance portfolio returns and achieve diversification. The hypothesis was that – due to a low correlation between common stock returns and REIT share returns, portfolios consisting of common stocks and REIT shares would show greater diversification benefits than portfolios consisting of either stocks or REITs alone. This issue was examined by comparing proximity and characteristics of efficient frontiers of portfolios consisting of either stocks, REITs or a combination of both. Efficient frontier proximity of mixed portfolios was found to be superior to those of single asset-type portfolios. It was concluded that REITs offered significant portfolio diversification benefits when compared to common stock portfolios. This phenomenon was based on the low return correlation of REITs with common stocks.

Another study focused on a portfolio of REITs over the period 1981–1986 and found that REITs reduced portfolio risk to a greater extent than a portfolio of common stocks. Although the findings were statistically significant, it concluded that REITs generally can perform well over a short time period, but it can become difficult to accurately measure long-term REIT performance in the context of a cyclically strong commercial real estate market.

Our Kuala Lumpur Roadshow 2019 where investors came to appreciate how REITs can be effective diversifiers of wealth.

> **LESSON LEARNED**
>
> The addition of REITs to a diversified common stock portfolio has proven to enhance an investment portfolio's returns and achieve diversification. REITs complement other types of investments by offering a defensive position during volatile market conditions. Because of the strong dividend income that REITs provide, they are an important investment both for passive income investors as well as retirees who require a continuing income stream to meet daily living expenses.

TRANSPARENT CORPORATE STRUCTURE

The REIT industry is required to report its DPU and results on a quarterly or half-yearly basis. In turn this has contributed to REITs as transparent corporate structures due to the quarterly or half-yearly assessments of their performance by a whole host of investment analysts, credit analysts, bankers and rating agencies.

As required by MAS law, REITs have to pay at least 90% of their earnings as dividends. Thus, a good measure of a REIT is how its DPU performed on a quarterly or semi-annual basis. This has been a great benchmark that I have used to analyse REITs.[1]

Against the backdrop of accounting fraud and irregularities from mainland Chinese companies listed on SGX, commonly known as S-chips from 2008 till 2014 and the collapse of small cap stocks like Blumont, Asiasons, Ipco which caused $8 billion in market capitalization to be wiped off in a single month in 2015 due to alleged manipulation, a REIT's transparent and stable structure is much appreciated and embraced by many investors.

A close study of REITs in the US, Australia, Japan, Hong Kong and Singapore has revealed that incidences of corporate fraud and irregularities are few and far in between in the past 60 years as the difficulty in hiding irregularities while needing to pay DPU on a cash basis every quarterly or semi-annually can be immense. Thus, a healthy DPU and DPU growth are crucial parameters to assess how good a REIT is. Whilst some REIT managers may hide behind a lackadaisical DPU or DPU growth for a few quarters, eventually for a REIT price to perform, a healthy DPU and good DPU growth rate are paramount.

---

1   "Singapore REITs – Replete With Splendour," *GCP Global*, 12/1/2020, https://gcpglobalsg.wixsite. com/gcpglobal/post/singapore-reits-replete-with-splendour; "The Ability to Deliver DPU Growth is the Key in SREITs Outperformance in 2018," *GCP Global*, 3/1/2019, https://gcpglobalsg.wixsite.com/ gcpglobal/post/the-ability-to-deliver-dpu-growth-is-the-key-in-sreits-outperformance-in-2018.

LESSON LEARNED

While there might be a few glitches to DPU and DPU growth, an essential feature of a good REIT is one that has a healthy DPU and good DPU growth. S-REITs that have been able to deliver steady DPU and consistent DPU growth have outperformed over the past two decades.

GCP Management Holdings student investors in Penang who are busy top medical specialists and surgeons appreciate the fact that REITs' transparent structure allows them to park their wealth safely while they are busy with their professional lives.

Chapter 4

ANALYSING REITS FOR OUTPERFORMANCE

This chapter is designed to provide investors with an understanding of the performance and valuation metrics required to evaluate REITs, together with various inputs in my personal encounters with the CEOs of REITs or their respective heads of investor relations over lunches, quarterly update meetings or investors meetings over the past two decades.

When used in good combination and sufficient market knowledge and experience, the investor will be able to unearth significant insights that separate the sheep from the goats among the REITs. The smart investor will get a good perspective of profitability, financial flexibility, dividend safety, management capability, and long-term prospects of the REITs.

Financial statements are typically audited annually by independent auditors and therefore a reliable source of updates on the financial health of a REIT. Used together with the quarterly statements, the smart and sharp REIT investor would be able to get an edge over others in understanding the direction and nuances of the REIT before the share price reflects that.

OPERATING PROFIT & LOSS METRICS
There are a number of different metrics used to determine the relative strengths and weaknesses of a REIT's operations.

Net Property Income (NPI)

A REIT is as good as the kind of properties it owns. How profitable a REIT is, eventually boils down to how its leases are structured. Investors looking for dividend sustainability should look at this segment in great detail.

$$
\begin{aligned}
\text{NPI} = \; & \text{Rental Revenue} + \\
& + \text{Tenant Reimbursement} \\
& - \text{All Property Expenses} \\
& - \text{Taxes} \\
& - \text{Insurance}
\end{aligned}
$$

Essentially, NPI measures the property-level profit on a stand-alone basis, excluding the REIT's corporate overheads or its financing strategies. The NPI is a very important metric used to value a REIT property as its earning power after deducting property-related expenses. It is also a very good indicator if a property has been bought or sold on an expensive or cheap basis. It is a very good measure of the fundamental attractiveness of the underlying properties in any REIT portfolio.

In general, the "safety" nature of investing in real estate and REITs lies in the relatively stable and predictable property-related revenues and expenses. Thus, the NPI is a good and reliable measure of a REIT's operating efficiency. Besides property-related expenses, NPI also incorporates management fees paid to the REIT manager, payment of trustee fees, interest cost of loans, audit and professional services fees and expenses. In addition, any earned income from interest placed in fixed deposits is also added back to NPI.

The NPI is a good indicator of a REIT's management track record. It is one good indicator that over time, better REITs management teams would be able to generate consistent above-average same-store growth. This ability to deliver same-store NPI growth will eventually be reflected in superior annual total returns to shareholders.

Assessing a management team's performance by comparing the last 5, 10 or 15 years of reported same-store NPI growth and annual total returns against that of their peers in the same industry, serves as a good benchmark for investors in ranking the management team's performance over the long-run.

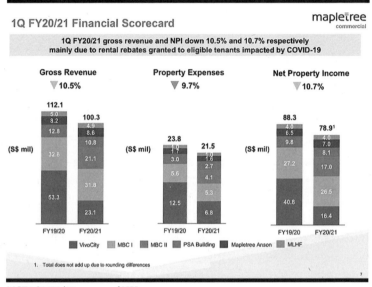

MCT 1Q2020/21 revenue and NPI

For instance, Mapletree Commercial Trust (MCT) has been a great performer since IPO. Its share price has more than doubled from its IPO price of $0.88 on April 2011 to $1.93 as at 30 June 2020. The share price alone has notched up a gain of 119.32% since IPO. Together with accumulated DPU of $0.344, MCT generated a Total Return of $1.394 or 158.41%. This translates to a CAGR of 12.60% over the past nine years. With a compounded growth rate greater than 10% per annum, investors in MCT would have doubled their investment capital every 7.5 years!

The above slide shows why MCT has been one of our favourite stocks in our REIT classes over the decade. MCT had been able to generate greater NPI with the recent acquisition of Mapletree Business City II while still maintaining the growth of NPI in its other properties, i.e. positive same-store sales. For instance, its prime VivoCity asset has been able to continuously post positive NPI growth year-on-year since its completion in 2006. Only COVID-19 put a dent to that as the REIT made provisions of $43.7 million to cater to its retail tenants at Vivo City for rental rebates.

Investors should always be wary of REITs that expand and acquire rapidly, while their existing assets suffer a decline in NPI. It normally begs the question if the managers had embarked on just acquisitions more so to help bridge the fall in NPI contribution from existing buildings as compared to the true merits of any new acquisition. As far as possible, investors should always ascertain if the "same-store sales" continue to be strong on existing assets. Naturally, if a REIT has been able to deliver on "same-store sales", investors would be more confident about future asset acquisitions by the REIT manager.

	IPO DATE	IPO PRICE	DPU till 2019	DPU 1Q2020	Total DPU	
MCT	27/04/2011	$0.88	$0.3349	0.0091	$0.3440	
	Price	%	Total Return		CAGR	
	30/06/2020	Change	$	%	Total	%
	$1.9300	219.32%	1.3940	158.41%	2.2740	12.60%

MCT's Share Price Return, Total Return and CAGR since IPO.

LESSON LEARNED

The safe nature of investing in real estate and REITs lies in the relatively stable and predictable property-related revenues and expenses. Thus, the NPI is a good and reliable measure of a REIT's operating efficiency. The NPI is also a good indicator of a REIT's management track record. It is one good indicator that over time, better REITs management teams would be able to generate consistent above-average same-store growth.

Net Property Income Yield (NPI Yield)

$$\text{NPI Yield} = \text{NPI}/\text{Revenue from property} \ (\%)$$

The NPI Yield is an important way to measure the future income of a REIT's property. The return you get now and in the future are key factors that REIT investors should take into account in assessing whether REITs are making right acquisitions or just adding to portfolios to increase their management fees.

The NPI Yield is calculated as a percentage, over the property's cost or market value, annual income and operating expenditures. When calculating NPI yields, it is important to distinguish between a gross yield and a net yield. The former is everything before expenses, whereas the latter accounts for all operating expenses, management fees, maintenance costs, stamp duties and vacancy costs. The difference in gross yield vs net yield can be rather stark for overseas properties, so REITs acquiring overseas properties should be scrutinized with greater care.

I have always stressed in all my REIT classes that the smart REIT investor should always calculate the NPI yield of properties, more so if they were bundled as a portfolio for acquisition. This is because the NPI represents actual cash flows paid by the tenant to the REIT. There is no assumption or pro forma figures involved. There are other methods of valuation based on recent transactions, capitalization rates comparison or replacement cost methods. However, the actual income method probably mirrors the actual valuation best.

For example, in CapitaLand Retail China's (CRCT) portfolio valuation of its China retail malls for year-end 2019, the average NPI Yield is 5.7% for its 13 malls, but the actual NPI Yield for its various malls range from a low of 4.2% for Rock Square to as high as 10.6% for CapitaMall Qibao. Even its three properties in Beijing, namely Xizhimen, Wangjing and Grand Canyon have a fairly wide valuation cap rate of 4.3% to 6.4%.

The differences in NPI Yield are a reflection of retail dynamics in the different regions in China, business confidence and occupancies. It is also a reflection of the population catchment area and the income growth of a particular geographic area or province.

For example, CRCT went ahead to acquire Rock Square Mall in Guangzhou at an NPI Yield of 3.7%. At first glance, it seemed that

Portfolio Valuation

CapitaLand

Category	Investment Property	Valuation (RMB Million)			As at 31 Dec 2019	
		As at 31 Dec 2019	As at 30 Jun 2019	Variance (%)	NPI Yield[1] (%)	Valuation psm of GRA (RMB)
Multi-Tenanted Malls	CapitaMall Xizhimen	3,580	3,453	3.7%	6.2%	43,094
	CapitaMall Wangjing	2,772	2,677	3.5%	6.4%	40,759
	CapitaMall Grand Canyon	2,125	2,111	0.7%	4.3%	30,371
	CapitaMall Xuefu	1,792	-	-	6.1%	17,182
	CapitaMall Xinnan	1,600	1,586	0.9%	6.2%	29,840
	CapitaMall Yuhuating	760	-	-	6.0%	12,975
	CapitaMall Aidemengdun	480	-	-	5.3%	11,061
	CapitaMall Qibao	435	459	(5.2)%	10.6%	5,981
	CapitaMall Minzhongleyuan	490	515	(4.9)%	N.M.[2]	11,746
	Rock Square[3]	3,425	3,403	0.6%	4.2%	40,973
Master-Leased Malls	CapitaMall Erqi	645	645	-	5.3%[4]	6,984
	CapitaMall Shuangjing	610	593	2.9%	6.2%	12,332
Held for Sale	CapitaMall Saihan[5]	460	460	-	8.9%	10,969
Under Fit-Out	Yuquan Mall	857	-	-	N.M.	11,231
Total Portfolio[6]		**20,031**	**15,902**	**26.0%**	**5.7%[7]**	

Notes:
1. NPI yield is based on NPI for FY 2019 and valuation as at 31 December 2019, except for CapitaMall Xuefu, CapitaMall Aidemengdun and CapitaMall Yuhuating where NPI yield is based on the annualised NPI for CRCT's holding period from 1 September 2019 to 31 December 2019. RMB16d adjustments are excluded in the NPI for CapitaMall Qibao, CapitaMall Minzhongleyuan and Rock Square.
2. CapitaMall Minzhongleyuan's NPI yield is not meaningful as the mall is under stabilisation.
3. CRCT has a 51.0% interest in Rock Square; valuations presented at 100% basis.
4. CapitaMall Erqi's FY 2019 NPI reflects only 10 months of revenue from the master lessee.
5. Excludes CapitaMall Wuhu as the mall has been divested in 10 Jul 2019.
6. Referring to agreed property selling price for CapitaMall Saihan as it is classified as asset held for sale.
7. Based on CRCT's effective interest of Rock Square and NPI basis stated in Note 1. Excludes Yuquan Mall as the asset is undergoing fitting-out.
N.M. – Not meaningful

18

CapitaLand Retail China's portfolio valuation of its China retail malls for year-end 2019

CRCT had acquired a low-yielding asset, but on further examination and querying the CEO, it became clear that strong demand for the property was a stronger driver for the low NPI Yield as that drove up the cost price of the property.

Investors should always assess a REIT's acquisition of new assets based on the likelihood of finding and retaining good assets with strong stream of tenants, suitability, demand-supply dynamics, location and future government plans for the region where the property is located.

REITs used to be more shareholder-friendly when they announced acquisitions and took pains to share such information above. However, with REITs embarking on portfolio acquisitions (which consists of many properties and many-a-times in different jurisdictions) rather than stand-alone buildings, this extent of information sharing has become less commonplace.

Instead, REITs embarking on portfolio acquisitions often choose to announce just a blended average NPI Yield which is a simple average of all the buildings targeted for acquisition. However, I find such announcements in relation to a key parameter rather liberal as an average number to reflect a transaction is really open to different interpretations.

Let me illustrate with a recent acquisition by Cromwell European REIT.

On 21 June 2019, Cromwell REIT announced its plans to acquire six properties for €246.9 million (S$380.6 million). Three of the properties were located in Grand Paris in France, two in Krakow, Poland and one in Poznan, Poland. The intra-day high share price before the announcement was €0.53.

Cromwell had previously failed to list in 2017 as its then proposed IPO portfolio consisted of several Polish assets that were considered riskier than its blended portfolio which included offices and warehouses in Germany, Netherlands, Denmark, Finland and Italy. Cromwell then subsequently did not include the Polish assets in the subsequent re-submission for its IPO which enabled them to list on November 2017 at €0.55.

Post-IPO, the acquisition on 21 June 2019 would raise Cromwell REIT's Polish exposure to 11.8% comprising six assets, from nil at IPO.

I am always wary of REITS that announce acquisitions as a package of assets because the overall blended figure may actually overshadow some of the underlying key parameters like Net Income Yield, NPI growth and DPU accretion, etc, of each of the individual assets.

For instance, Cromwell's latest acquisitions on 21 June 2019 came with a very attractive net initial yield of 7.4% which was substantially higher than the 5.8% enjoyed by its existing office portfolio at first glance. A closer analysis will reveal that Cromwell's two Krakow assets boasted initial yield of 7.5% while the Poznan freehold property achieved an even more impressive initial yield of 8.0%. This clearly implies that the three Paris assets, the more prized assets, were acquired at below 7.15% NPI yield then! The Paris assets were in fact acquired at an NPI yield of 6.5%, a full 1.5% lower than the Poznan asset. Thus, the sharp and smart REIT investor should take note of the huge difference in NPI yields amongst the various properties in the acquisition portfolio, although the portfolio as a whole at 7.4% NPI yield looks impressive at first glance.

	Purchase Price	NPI Yield	Weighted Average	No. of Properties
Paris	$78.90	6.50%	2.07%	3
Krakow	$80.00	7.50%	2.42%	2
Poznan	$88.80	8.00%	2.87%	1
	$247.70		7.36%	

Cromwell REIT's acquisitions of 21 June 2019

On closer analysis, the Cap Mermoz property in Greater Paris actually has an NPI yield of 6.1% while the two other properties in Paryseine and Lenine yield 6.8%. The latter two are actually not your typical Grade A office properties, but are three-level warehouses which obviously are of higher risk. Thus, not surprisingly, their NPI yields are nearer 7%.

Cromwell undertook a massive 328.086 million private placement of shares to raise €150 million to fund these acquisitions on 21 June 2019. Minority shareholders who were not offered the private placement at €0.46 would have been diluted as the private placement price was at a large discount of 9.6% (by far the largest discount compared to all other REIT private placements in 2019) to its then Volume Weighted Average Price (VWAP) of €0.5091 for the preceding market day on 20 June 2019. This discount is even wider at 11.7% to the VWAP of 0.5209 including married trades done on 20 June 2019.

The 21 June 2019 acquisition and fund raising was Cromwell's 5th and 2nd respectively after its listing in November 2017. By all accounts, Cromwell has grown its portfolio size since IPO to 103 properties worth €2.042 billion upon the completion of the acquisition vs 74 properties worth €1.354 billion at IPO. This is a whopping 51% growth in less than two years! The pertinent question to the smart and sharp REIT investor should be: Have the benefits of the acquisitions filtered down to the DPU where he/she can then benefit? Also, the share price has a very high correlation with the DPU trend. While the share price can act like a voting machine in the short run, it will act as a weighing machine for the merits of the growth strategy that a REIT has undertaken in the long run.

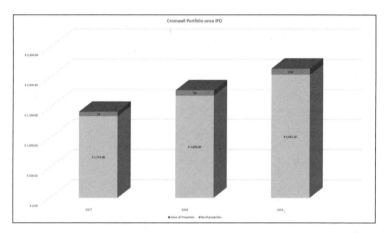

Cromwell has grown its portfolio since IPO to 103 properties worth €2.042 billion upon the completion of the acquisition vs 74 properties worth €1.354 billion at IPO.

Hardly has the dust settled from the last purchase before another begins. For the sagacious REIT investor, it is vital to assess each acquisition to see if indeed the various acquisitions enhance DPU as what the REIT's pre-acquisition presentation deck had communicated. Investors should specifically look out to what extent do the acquisitions enhance DPU.

Cromwell's share price has wallowed below its IPO price of €0.55 ever since and ended 2019 at €0.54. The share price briefly exceeded its €0.55 IPO price on 30 November 2017 for a brief period. It then briefly traded above its IPO price again in 1Q2020 before plunging down to less than €0.30 during the COVID-19 crisis sell-off. Thus, it has traded below its IPO price for almost the rest of the two years and seven months since it was listed. It closed at €0.42 as at 30 June 2020. For outperformance, the smart and sharp REIT investor should always be watchful of REITs that will underperform over specific periods of time as long term underperformance can result in a huge difference in terminal wealth.

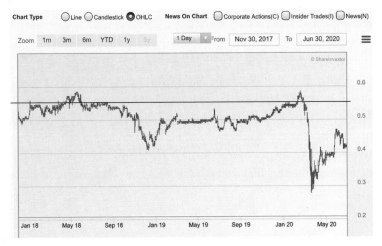

Cromwell REIT price since IPO in November 2017 – price has traded below its IPO price of €0.55 for most of the time in the past two years and seven months since it was listed. Source: ShareInvestor

---

LESSON LEARNED

For the smart REIT investor, it is vital to assess each acquisition to see if indeed the various individual assets enhance DPU or whether the acquisitions are only accretive on an average blended basis which is normally what is highlighted in the REIT's acquisition presentation announcement. This is to further understand if the higher-risk assets are packaged together with good acquisitions which will naturally boost NPI yield.

Interest Cover

Interest Cover is calculated as –
(Earnings Before Interest, Taxes, Depreciation and Amortization, EBITDA) / Total Interest Costs

The Interest Cover measures how many times earnings exceed the interest expense incurred on loans drawn down to finance the REIT's property. It is directly affected by the income generating ability of the property and the interest expense incurred to finance the property. It is a good measure when used together with the Gearing Ratio to encapsulate the financial position of a REIT as well as to measure how easily or difficult the REIT can repay its interest expense on outstanding debt.

All REITs thrive on financing, the cheaper the better. Naturally therefore, the Interest Cover is a good indication to investors as to how far a REIT can gear up further and also indicates if a REIT is ramping up acquisitions too quickly. It also indicates to investors that when interest rates change suddenly, which are the REITs (obviously the highly-geared ones) that would be most vulnerable in terms of share price volatility.

REITs with good Interest Cover are a result of either lower gearing of the balance sheet, better-income generation ability of its property or better reputation of the sponsor that allowed the REIT to secure bank financing at lower interest rates.

Whilst there is no clear optimal Interest Cover for a REIT, past performances have indicated that those with the strongest Interest Cover like Keppel DC REIT and Parkway Life REIT, have done well and consistently outperform the other REITs with lower Interest Cover.

INTEREST COVER					
	31-Dec-18	31-Mar-19	30-Jun-19	30-Sep-19	31-Dec-19
Parkway Life REIT	13.50	13.20	13.80	14.30	14.10
Keppel DC REIT	11.20	12.90	12.90	12.70	13.30

Strong Interest Cover has been the backbone of great performances for both REITs

Keppel DC REIT has been a great performer since IPO. We told our students who attended our Saturday, 13 August 2016 REITs class that Keppel DC REIT was reaching a turning point (REIT price was then $1.14) since its IPO as the structure of the lease, the lengthened WALE (weighted average lease expiry), the strong Interest Cover, the price paid for its acquisitions, and the quality of assets were the kind that would propel share price and DPU growth.

Since then, the share price speaks for itself as it has continued to soar to $2.55 as at 30 June 2020.

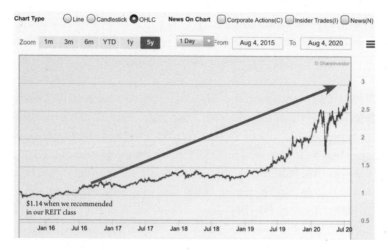

Chart Type   ○Line ○Candlestick ●OHLC   News On Chart   ○Corporate Actions(C) ○Insider Trades(I) ○News(N)

The lengthened WALE, the strong Interest Cover and the structure of the lease propelled Keppel DC share price since we presented the stock at $1.14 in our Quarterly REITs class on 13 August 2016. Source: ShareInvestor.

As mentioned in the Operating Balance Sheet section, the accounting board has allowed REITs to classify 50% of Perpetual Equity raised by REITs to be classified as Equity and the other 50% as long-term debt. Thus, in calculating the interest cover, investors should account for any interest expense from perpetuals as these are expenses that the REIT should service. They should be incorporated into the interest cover calculation.

While there is no definitive number on what the interest cover quantitatively should be, in practice, the better-performing REITs have interest cover far higher than the industry average. The quarterly and interim results of REITs offer a good source of checking the interest cover for any significant change, especially in volatile times when interest rates are on an up climb. Many smaller REITs (as compared to the larger REITs or those with good sponsors) tend to be affected by a deterioration in the interest cover during such times which will have an adverse impact on their share prices.

Dividend Per Unit (DPU)

DPU = Total Dividend Payout / Number of Shares

The DPU is the sum of all the quarterly or semi-annual dividends. It is the metric that has consistently ranked as Number 1 for investors to invest in REITs. Thus, the smart investor should always pay close attention to all the numbers that lead up to the calculation of the DPU and the way it is being reported. It is one of the best metrics to assess the profitability and health of a REIT and spot any underperformers.

As in our quarterly REITs class, we have always highlighted that the ability of S-REITs to deliver outperformance should not be based on growth in revenue or NPI or Distributable Income, but on the DPU.[1]

The 2018 set of REIT results clearly confirmed our assertion. Assessments of the top and worst performing REITs in the past decade on a year-on-year basis, has also underscored what we have been teaching about the DPU as a great measure of REIT performance.

An increase in gross revenue and NPI should always come with an increase in DPU. DPU is how much an investor gets for every unit they own of the REIT. A jump in gross revenue and NPI without a corresponding increase in DPU could mean that the REIT has issued new units priced at sharp discounts to raise funds. Most S-REITs have always justified their acquisitions as yield-accretive, but investors should be looking for DPU-accretive. It is our contention that if a REIT has to resort to cheap fund raising via deeply-discounted rights or a placement of shares to fund an acquisition, the transaction should not be consummated as it erodes shareholders' interest. Throughout my experience, I have not seen many REIT acquisitions, financed by cheap rights or placement shares, do well in their share price.

---

1   "The Ability to Deliver DPU Growth is the Key in SREITs Outperformance in 3Q2017," *GCP Global*, 18/12/2017, https://gcpglobalsg.wixsite.com/gcpglobal/post/the-ability-to-deliver-dpu-growth-is-the-key-in-sreits-outperformance-in-3q2017; "The Ability to Deliver DPU Growth is the Key in SREITs Outperformance in 2018," *GCP Global*, 3/1/2019, https://gcpglobalsg.wixsite.com/gcpglobal/post/the-ability-to-deliver-dpu-growth-is-the-key-in-sreits-outperformance-in-2018.

Un-interrupted Recurring DPU Growth Since IPO

❑ DPU has grown steadily at a rate of 108.7%[1] since IPO

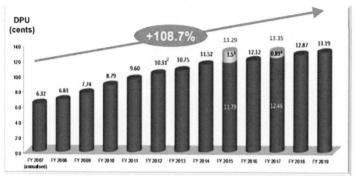

Note
1.   Since IPO till YTD 4Q 2019
2.   Since FY2012, S$3.0 million per annum of amount available for distribution has been retained for capital expenditure
3.   One-off divestment gain of 1.50 cents (S$9.11 million) relating to the divestment of seven Japan assets in December 2014 was equally
      distributed over the four quarters in FY2015
4.   One-off divestment gain of 0.89 cents (S$5.39 million) relating to the divestment of four Japan assets in December 2016 was equally
      distributed over the four quarters in FY2017

Parkway Life REIT has posted steady DPU growth since IPO

Instead, I have seen REITs that grow their assets well and only embark on careful accretive acquisitions steadily, do well in their share price.

The above shows Parkway Life REIT DPU growth since IPO. It is noteworthy that Parkway Life started life with only three assets in Singapore, namely Gleneagles Hospital, Mount Elizabeth Hospital and East Shore Hospital and two nursing homes in Japan.

Thirteen years after its IPO, the three namesake hospitals still constitute more than 60% of its total portfolio of close to $2 billion and contribute more than 60% of NPI which has now grown to include more than 40 nursing homes in Japan. What is clear from the DPU chart above is that Parkway Life REIT has been able to deliver steady and consistent DPU growth since its IPO from almost the same asset base acquired at IPO. In turn, it has been rewarded by steady and consistent growth in its share price which has soared from its IPO price of $1.28 in Aug 2007 to $3.34 as at 30 June 2020. Including cumulative dividends of $1.297 (which alone is already higher than the IPO price), the total returns achieved by Parkway Life REIT is a whopping $3.423 or 267.42% return over 12 years. This translates into a CAGR of 11.45%!

Good Recurring DPU growth has propelled Parkway Life REIT price up steadily since IPO. Source: ShareInvestor.

LESSON LEARNED

The huge divergence in performance between the Worst Performing REITs and the Top Performing REITS over the decades, clearly illustrate that those REITS that do not appreciate the needs of REIT investors looking for steady and consistent returns via DPU, have and will not do well. REIT managers can have excuses and attribute lower DPUs to higher interest expenses or what-not, but if they do not deliver positive DPU growth, the REIT price will suffer along with the investors.

Dividend or DPU Yield

DPU Yield = (Annualized DPU/REIT Share Price) * 100%

The dividend or DPU Yield is a good benchmark for comparison of REITs within the same sector as well as to compare over time. As it is dependent on the volatility of the underlying share price, it could be a good indicator of the REIT's attractiveness because if the yield goes up, it would mean that inversely, the share price had come down and vice versa.

More importantly, the dividend yield is a critical element in calculating the yield spread.

Yield Spread

Yield Spread = Dividend or DPU Yield – Risk-free Rate

The yield spread is an indicator of the risk premium when investing in a REIT as compared to the risk-free rate which is normally proxied by the respective country's 10-year bond yield.

Most textbooks and analysts have made their judgment calls based on yield spread in the following context:

If the yield spread narrows, is decreasing or becomes negative, this implies that the REIT has become expensive

Whereas

If the yield spread widens, is increasing or turning from negative to positive, this implies that the REIT is turning out to be a good buy.

However, in practice in the S-REITs market, theory has not turned out to be practical. Instead, the market has often behaved in the opposite way.

LESSON LEARNED

The better-performing REITs tend to show a disciplined and well-thought through strategy in running their business which is shown clearly through the Profit & Loss statement and the financial strength and flexibility in its Balance Sheet.

The better-performing REITs in the past two decades have been able to exhibit an increasing DPU growth profile, despite capital raising via placements or rights issue. Also, the better-performing REITs have balance sheets that are not unduly geared, have strong interest covers and are able to borrow from banks at competitive interest rates. WALEs are longer and debt maturities are well-spaced out to avoid refinancing shocks arising from events like the GFC or when interest rates start to move up.

OPERATING BALANCE SHEET METRICS

REITs, more so than other kinds of business, are heavily dependent on the debt market cycle, the interest cost and the ability to raise financing from their shareholders. Thus, for the perspicacious REIT investor, all these items are important in assessing the balance sheet of the REIT to help determine its financing needs. Increasingly, in the past five years when REITs have undertaken close to $35 billion in new acquisitions, it has become apparent that REITs that have used financing structures friendly to minority shareholders with minimal dilution, have done well compared to those REITs that have resorted to raising new capital at huge discounts.

Balance Sheet

The balance sheet reflects the REIT's financial condition and provides a financial snapshot at any moment of time. Essentially, it is

$$Equity = Assets - Liabilities$$
$$Assets = Liabilities + Equity$$

Broadly, assets are divided into current assets and long-term assets.

Current assets are those possessions owned by the REIT that can be converted into cash in a short time frame, typically in less than a year. These normally comprise cash, bank deposits and accounts receivables.

Long-term assets which are also commonly-known as non-current assets are possessions held for more than one business cycle or one year. They are typically the REIT's investment properties and property, plant and equipment.

Similar to assets, liabilities are also divided into current liabilities and long-term liabilities.

Current liabilities are debts which the REIT needs to pay within one business cycle or the next 12 months. These include accounts payable and taxes.

Non-current liabilities are debts due beyond 12 months or one business cycle. The most common include long-term debts and bonds.

In recent years, the accounting board has allowed REITS to classify 50% of Perpetual Equity raised by REITs to be classified as equity and the other 50% as long-term debt.

Equity is generally classified into Issued Capital and Retained Earnings. It represents the shareholders' interest. As mentioned above, the accounting board has allowed REITs to classify 50% of Perpetual Equity raised by REITs to be classified as equity and the other 50% as long-term debt. However, we have always taught in class that for the conservative REIT investor, it is always best to classify 100% of Perpetual Equity as debt.

Distribution Statement

The Distribution Statement is also commonly known as the Statement of Funds Available for Distribution and a good source of understanding the reliability of a REIT's DPU.

$$\text{Distributable Income} = \text{Net Income} + \text{Non-cash Expenses} - \text{Non-cash Income}$$

The difference in the distributable income and net income is the nature of non-cash items which include depreciation, amortization, cost of forex hedge, gains or losses from revaluation gains and management fees paid in units.

In recent years, many REITs have alluded that because they take their management fees in units instead of in cash, their interests are aligned with that of minority shareholders. I find such statements rather shallow and difficult to understand as management fees are still paid to the REIT managers. No discount to the total fee amount is given and the managers can sell these units in the future with no time moratorium.

What the smart and sharp REIT investor should pay attention to is the gain and losses from revaluation gains of the REIT's properties as they are one of the earliest indicators of either over-payment by REIT managers for the purchase of assets (which no manager will admit and will be an event that will only be known later) or the margin of safety that managers bring to bear on their asset acquisition strategies.

Gearing

Gearing Ratio = Total Debt/Total Asset * 100%

The Gearing Ratio is the total debt over the total asset of the REIT. The fundamental operation of a REIT is that the manger undertakes loans and issues new equity to buy assets, lease the assets and collect rental from the assets. Dividends are essentially paid from profits which are distributed after meeting expenses like interest charges, management fees, insurance and other fees. Therefore, the gearing ratio is one of the most important considerations for a REIT as it shapes the debt profile and susceptibility to volatile capital market conditions. A REIT with excessive debt would have interest expenses that could possibly erode bottom line growth. From the S-REIT experience, flirting with the maximum gearing ratio can leave the share price vulnerable on the downside when the capital market changes, as what COVID-19 has shown again. The same behaviour was borne out during the Global Financial Crisis of 2007 to 2009.[2]

REITS	Share Price	Share Price	Price	%	Gearing as	Gearing as
	Wed 19th Feb	Mon 23rd Mar	Change	Change	31-Dec-19	31-Mar-20
OUE Comm REIT	$0.520	$0.290	-$0.230	-44.23%	40.30%	39.30%
ARA Logos Log	$0.710	$0.360	-$0.350	-49.30%	40.10%	40.80%
ESR-REIT	$0.545	$0.240	-$0.305	-56.00%	41.50%	41.70%
Lippo Malls	$0.225	$0.107	-$0.118	-52.44%	35.90%	41.70%
ARA Hospitality	$0.860	$0.320	-$0.540	-62.79%	32.10%	41.00%

The gearing ratio is one of the most important considerations for a REIT as it shapes the debt profile and susceptibility to volatile capital market conditions.

The above table shows the five REITs with the highest gearing ratio going into the COVID-19 sell-off. OUE Commercial REIT, ARA

---

2   "Financial Advice for 2009", *The Sunday Times*, 28 December 2008.

Logos Logistics and ESR-REIT had gearing already exceeding the 40% limit as at end-December 2019. The REIT prices fell a whopping 44.23% to 56.00% in just 22 days of sell-off. This compares to an average of 38% drop for the MACFK REITs (Mapletree, Ascendas, CapitaLand, Frasers and Keppel group REITs) for the same period.

Lippo Malls which saw its net asset value plummet, leading to an increase in its gearing ratio to 41.7% in its 1Q2020 results, fell 52.44%. Newly-listed ARA US Hospitality Trust undertook an acquisition of three premium Marriott-branded Select Service hotels in Raleigh and San Antonio worth a total of US$84.5 million on 6 November 2019 and financed the acquisition wholly by bank borrowings. This proved to be most untimely as falling asset values on an enhanced asset base on higher borrowings sent gearing up to 41.00% come their 1Q2020 results. The smart and sharp REIT investor would have anticipated that as the share price took a 62.79% dive, the second largest drop (the worst being Eagle Hospitality Trust before its suspension) in the S-REIT sector for the period of 19 February 2020 to 23 March 2020.

Clearly, the gearing ratio has proven to be one of the most important considerations for a REIT as it shapes the debt profile and susceptibility to volatile capital market conditions as what the COVID-19 sell-off has shown. REITs should leave a generous buffer from the maximum gearing ratio as that can leave the share price vulnerable on the downside when the capital market changes in a short space of time.

ESR-REIT is a great example – when it deftly redeemed and cancelled its $130 million 3.95% Series 004 Notes in May 2020, which brought down its gearing quickly, the share price sharply recovered 64.58% to close at 39.5 cents by end-June 2020. It certainly took home the accolade for one of the sharpest rebounds for an S-REIT and exemplifies that if one undertakes the right action in a timely manner (a reflection of astute management), the share price will react commensurately and almost immediately.

Effective from 2016, the gearing ratio has been capped at 45%. In practice, most REITs have kept their gearing ratios to less than 40% as a gearing of close to 45% would imply limited room for further borrowings to fund future expansion, normally known as the debt headroom. MAS has raised the leverage ratio for S-REITs from 45% to 50%, to provide S-REITS with greater flexibility to manage their capital structure created by the COVID-19 pandemic in April 2020.

Obviously, REITs with the lowest gearing would have the greatest flexibility in future expansion with a stronger debt headroom.

Also, as REITs need to revalue their properties on a yearly basis, any downward revaluation of its properties will result in lower asset values. This will then increase the gearing of the REIT. This effect becomes more pronounced during an asset down cycle or economic recession or slowdown. Very often, the share price of REITs will react sharply to such events, thus the smart and sharp REIT investor should always be anticipating such a possibility.

In certain circumstances, REITs may be forced to sell its other assets to pare down gearing and/or pay its debt. This would have serious consequences for its share price.

As mentioned earlier, the accounting board has allowed REITS to classify 50% of Perpetual Equity raised by REITs to be classified as equity and the other 50% as long-term debt. However, we have always taught in class that for the conservative REIT investor, it is always best to classify 100% of Perpetual Equity as debt.

LESSON LEARNED

Investors should always pay close attention to the gearing of REITs as in practice, REITs which are managed such that their gearing ratios are flirting with the maximum statutory levels, have been shown to underperform vs those REITs that are more conservatively managed. Very often, the share price of REITs will react sharply to events that will affect a REIT's gearing, be it an anticipation of interest rate increases or asset down cycle. Thus, the smart and sharp REIT investor should always be anticipating such a possibility and react before such events impact the share price.

Chapter 5

HOW MUCH TO PAY FOR A REIT?

A REIT's value is the collection of all its properties within its portfolio. Thus, how much to pay for a REIT intuitively begs the question of how much to pay for the value of all its assets plus a premium or discount for the REIT manager's expertise and the strength of its sponsor.

In addition, there are a few other factors that affect how much a smart and sharp investor should pay for a REIT at any moment in time. Broadly, there are two approaches in valuing a REIT – the yield-based approach and the asset-backed approach.

In this chapter, we delve into these in great detail and address how much a sagacious investor should pay for a REIT at any moment in time, which I find in most research reports to be lacking or are ambiguous about.

Admittedly, valuing a REIT is part-science and part-art. However, honed with 31 years of direct experience in the financial sector as Head of Research, working in Wall Street, and then running the institutional sales desks in various financial institutions, I must admit that the rich experience greatly helped in sharpening my skills as a REIT investor. In this respect, the direct and appropriate experience has helped me understand deeper what drives a REIT's valuation and when to buy and sell.

YIELD-BASED APPROACH

The unique thing about REITs is that they offer steady dividends and potential for capital gain in the share price. For me, the relative stability and higher dividend as a percentage of Total Return feature of REITs gives me great comfort in investing. For instance, even if the share price of the REIT does not move, there is hardly any opportunity cost as S-REITs (unless you have picked a Value Trap REIT) have paid between 4.2% to 9.3% in yearly dividends in the past decade. This rate is higher than that of most AAA-bonds or the Singapore 10-year bond yield or dividend yields of most blue-chip stocks.

The starting point for any yield-based valuation approach is obviously the risk-free rate. This is essentially the interest rate that you get from investing in any financial product where the principal or capital value is protected. In Singapore, the Singapore 10-year bond yield is normally used as the risk-free rate. As REITs, like equities, are more volatile than government bonds, expected yields demanded by investors are naturally higher.

The question is how much?

The answer to this question rests on –

1.   DPU growth of the REIT
2.   Quality of DPU growth of the REIT
3.   REIT manager's track record
4.   Quality of the sponsor
5.   Portfolio and sector exposure
6.   Investors' perception of how well-run the REIT is

REIT yields are highly susceptible to market sentiment and volatility. As discussed in Chapter 4, a lot of bloggers and analysts got their timing wrong in calling for a peak in prices for REITs and thus recommended a SELL in April to June 2019 when we had maintained our BUY calls as REIT yields went to -2 standard deviation from the mean while Price/ Book Value went to +2 standard deviation from the mean.[1]

We maintained our BUY calls as we took into account a few conceptual flaws that many bloggers and market analysts make when they do their predictions. Many predictions were wrong as the S-REIT market established a new benchmark at +2 standard deviation from the mean before S-REITs peaked in May 2013 before a correction took place. This has subsequently become the benchmark to gauge if S-REITs have become expensive. It was used successfully in 2017

1   "The Most Overlooked Trait of Investing Success in REITs – Mastering Market Timing," *GCP Global*, 1/10/2019, https://gcpglobalsg.wixsite.com/gcpglobal/post/the-most-overlooked-trait-of-investing-success-in-reits-mastering-market-timing.

after the longest rally from August 2015 to December 2017 to call for a correction in 2018 which occurred at the same time when interest rates were raised three times.

Most predictions have failed in the past as the financial forecasters making them had used previous benchmarks rather than to ascertain if indeed, this benchmark is still relevant or if a newer benchmark is achievable now. After all, studying the longer history and trading patterns of the US REITs since 1961, the A-REIT in Australia since 1971 and the J-REIT market in Japan since 2001 would reveal that as the US REIT, A-REIT and J-REIT markets developed, the benchmarks for each cycle in terms of Yield and Price/Book Value were not arbitrary benchmarks, but rather evolving benchmarks. The perspicacious REIT investor must recognize that relative-yield valuation benchmarks change constantly with prices and prices can have a feedback loop back to valuation benchmarks.

When I was interviewed by the *Nikkei Asian Review* on 2 June 2019, I was of the view that most analysts and bloggers were making a mistake calling for SELLs on REITs in April and May 2019 as they had relied on historical benchmarks.[2] It is crucial to evaluate the impact of recent acquisitions which have positive impact on REITs DPU which in-turn will change valuation benchmarks. Also, relative yield valuation methods will change in different interest rate environments. Thus, ultra-low interest rates will be supportive of relative yield benchmarks stretching their previous highs.

For instance, Ascendas India Trust, Keppel DC REIT, Mapletree Industrial Trust, Mapletree Logistics Trust and Mapletree Commercial Trust had all shot pass their +2 standard deviation of their DPU Yield by May-2019. And they all ended up as the strongest performing stocks for 2019. Those who called SELLs on them were downright wrong as even when they surpassed the +2 standard deviation of their DPU Yield much further by May 2019, they continued to edge higher in the next seven months. The opportunity cost to selling these REITs in May 2019, without including dividends, ranged from 16.01% to 29.01% in just seven months. Clearly, when to take profits in REITs is as much an art as a science.

---

2   "Stellar rally puts valuations of Singapore REITs in focus," *Nikkei Asian Review*, 11/7/2019, https://asia.nikkei.com/Business/Markets/Nikkei-Markets/Stellar-rally-puts-valuations-of-Singapore-REITs-in-focus.

> **LESSON LEARNED**
>
> REIT valuation is part-science and part-art. The smart and sharp REIT investor should always reconcile the conditions where conventional valuation benchmarks no longer become a good guide and when to let their REITs run to enjoy more profits and capital gain. This is key in making your millions in REITs!

PRICE/BOOK VALUE (P/BV) OR PRICE/NET ASSET VALUE (P/NAV)

P/BV = Share Price of REIT/(Total Assets − Total Liabilities) per unit

As REITs are asset heavy in nature, the P/BV serves as a good indicator of how much an investor is paying for the underlying net asset of the REIT at any moment in time.

The P/BV or P/NAV is a good measure to assess if the REIT manager is prudent in the allocation of shareholder capital. NAV or Book Value measures the current market value of the REIT's properties and if the REIT manager had been acquiring well, valuations of the underlying asset should steadily increase and show up in the NAV or Book Value.

REITs whose shares trade at a premium to Book Value have a serious competitive advantage as they can continue to buy or develop assets to grow their portfolios. In contrast, if a REIT's shares are trading at a significant discount to NAV, management should shrink its portfolio by selling the least performing assets or lowest growth assets to pare down their debts. If not, they should embark on buying back their shares below book value, although this has to be balanced with the view of not increasing its total gearing or lead to a deterioration of its interest coverage ratio. A good example is Keppel REIT which used a fairly balanced approach in buying back their shares when it traded substantially below its P/BV while managing its interest coverage ratios and gearing ratios well.

REITs which enjoy trading at a huge premium to its book value or NAV do so due to multi-faceted reasons. It could be due to the fact that the property sector they are in are in favour or that seasoned investors rank their REIT manager highly. It could also be due to the fact that the REIT has a strong sponsor like the MACFK REITs[3] that we have been recommending in our REITs classes in the past decade. Alternatively, the premium may indicate that the shares are overvalued.

Again, most textbooks and analysts have made judgment calls on P/BV in the following context:

If the P/BV narrows, is decreasing or become less than 1, this implies that the REIT has become cheaper

Whereas

If the P/BV expands, is increasing or turning from -1 to +1, this implies that the REIT has become more expensive

However, in practice, going by the S-REITs market experience, theory has not turned out to be practical. Instead, often enough, the market behaved the opposite way. Some of the best-performing REITs have high P/BV or rising NAVs from either rising asset valuations and more accretive acquisitions or both.

BEST PERFORMING REITS 2013–2019	Share Price 31/12/2013	Share Price 31/12/2019	Price Change	% Change	NAV 31/12/2019	P/NAV 31/12/2019
Mapletree Commercial	$1.190	$2.390	$1.200	100.84%	1.70	1.41
Mapletree Industrial	$1.345	$2.600	$1.255	93.31%	1.51	1.72
Mapletree Logistics	$1.040	$1.740	$0.700	67.31%	1.17	1.49
Frasers Centrepoint Trust	$1.770	$2.810	$1.040	58.76%	2.21	1.27
CapitaComm Trust	$1.450	$1.990	$0.540	37.24%	1.81	1.10
AVERAGE						1.40

Top-5 performing REITs in the past six years and their rising P/NAV values

The above table shows the top-5 performing REITs in the past six years. The top-performer, Mapletree Commercial Trust (MCT)

3   "Singapore REITs – A Magnificent Run, Spearheaded By the MACFK," *GCP Global*, 3/7/2019, https://gcpglobalsg.wixsite.com/gcpglobal/post/singapore-reits-a-magnificent-run-spearheaded-by-the-macfk.

traded at a P/NAV of 1.406 at end-2019 while the average P/NAV of the Top-5 worked out to a 40% premium to book value.

Smart REIT investors should go further and spot corresponding rise in P/NAV of the 2nd Best Performer, namely, Mapletree Industrial Trust (MIT). The bulk of the share price rise in MIT occurred at the same time when the NAV was rising from 1.20 in 2013 to 1.51 in 2019. Correspondingly, the P/NAV rose steadily from 1.18 in 2013 to 1.72 at end-2019.

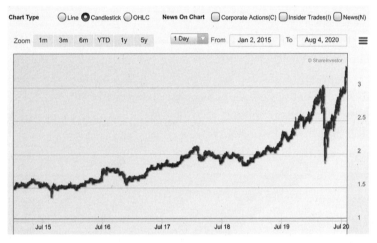

For MIT, more than 100% share price rise occurred at the same time when the P/NAV rose from 1.08 in 2013 to 1.72 at end-2019. Source: ShareInvestor.

Once again, what is taught in theory, differs from the practical world. The faster recovery in the prices of REITs with higher P/BV or P/NAV during the COVID-19 crisis confirms once again that investors are more willing to pay for the better managed REITs.

> **LESSON LEARNED**
>
> Markets tend to pay a premium for REITs with good management teams and strong sponsors that undertake acquisitions with financing structure that are favourable to minority shareholders. The other common factors amongst those REITs that outperform are those whose managers have consistently added value through rigorous and careful property management, and undertake smart AEIs (Asset Enhancement Initiative) that achieve good NPI yields.

Conversely, if a REIT trades at a sharp discount to its NAV or book value, it could be a reflection of the down cycle faced by the REIT in its property sector or the market's view that the REIT's assets are sub-par or manager or sponsor is destroying shareholder value, in which case the shares are cheap for a reason and should be avoided.

WORST PERFORMING REITS 2013–2019	Share Price 31/12/2013	Share Price 31/12/2019	Price Change	% Change	NAV 31/12/2019	P/NAV 31/12/2019
Sabana REIT	$1.080	$0.470	-$0.610	-56.48%	$0.56	0.84
Lippo Malls	$0.415	$0.225	-$0.190	-45.78%	$0.30	0.75
Cache Logistics	$1.120	$0.715	-$0.405	-36.16%	$0.56	1.28
Soilbuild Business REIT	$0.760	$0.525	-$0.235	-30.92%	$0.62	0.85
OUE Commercial REIT	$0.800	$0.560	-$0.240	-30.00%	$0.61	0.92
AVERAGE						0.93

Worst-5 performing REITs in the past six years and their P/NAV values

The above table shows the worst-5 performing REITs in the past six years. All, except for one, namely Cache Logistics, (currently known as ARA Logos Logistics) traded at a discount to their P/NAV and the average P/NAV of the worst-5 performing REITs in the past six years, worked out to 0.93 or a 7% discount to book value at end-2019.

Smart REIT investors should go further and spot a distinctive corresponding fall in P/NAV of Soilbuild Business Space REIT with its share price from 2015 to present. It coincided closely with the huge fall in its share price from a high of $0.865 in 2015 to $0.525 at end-2019 as its P/NAV turned from positive to negative during this period and ended at P/NAV of 0.85 or a discount of 15% at end-2019.

Once again, what is taught in theory, differs from the practical world. This is key in making your millions in REITs!

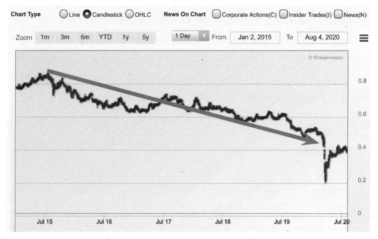

The huge fall in Soilbuild REIT share price from $0.865 in 2015 to $0.525 as at end-2019. This coincided with its P/NAV turning from positive to negative and ended at P/NAV of 0.847 or a discount of 15.3% at end-2019. Source: ShareInvestor.

LESSON LEARNED

The smart and sharp REIT investor should always stay clear of REITs that hardly enhance shareholder value and/or are value traps as the opportunity cost is just too high. Investors will miss out on good dividends and good capital growth if they had invested instead, into a good REIT that can deliver steady and consistent returns.

DIVIDEND DISCOUNT MODEL (DDM)

Both the yield-based approach and the P/BV or P/NAV approaches are relative valuation methodologies that try to derive the valuation relative to the yield behaviour or how the P/BV behaves, relative to its peers and over a period of time for comparison purposes.

The DDM seeks to determine the intrinsic value (IV) of the REIT. It is the summation of all future DPUs discounted to present value. Intuitively, as REITs tend to pay more stable DPU compared to equities, the DDM should be a more accurate method of valuation, but in practice, again this has not been the case.

In today's world, the volatile markets have called on analysts to make accurate forecasts of rental expenses and revenue based on rental rates, reversionary rental rates and occupancies. This goes into estimating the growth rate used in the DDM. As forecasts involve many variables which are sensitive to changing conditions in the DDM, variations of any one will significantly affect outcomes. A slight change in the DPU or growth rate used in DDM calculations can throw up a wide range of values of fair price for the REIT.

In reality, it is both difficult and simplistic to summarize into one figure the growth rate and dividend to be used in the DDM calculations. The analyst needs to incorporate property-specific factors which in turn, require a deep understanding of the macro factors and property dynamics affecting both demand and supply in different geographical areas where the properties are located.

Thus, in our classes, we have always taught that the DDM, detailed though it may be, may not be an accurate way for valuing a REIT as there are too many assumptions involved. And the multi-varied assumptions cannot be simplified into just a few numbers that become the variables in the DDM calculation. Also, slight changes of a few key variables can throw out a wide range in prices.

CAPITALIZATION RATIO (CAP RATE)

$$\text{Cap Rate} = \text{NPI or NOI/Property Value} * 100\%$$

The cap rate seeks to measure the NPI yield of the property.

The cap rate is also a good measurement of the relative attractiveness of one property compared to another in the same area or grade. It also gives an indication if a REIT manager has overpaid for a property or gotten a good deal.

REITs normally show details on the cap rate and at what price each of the property is valued at the middle or year-end of each financial year. This information is useful in helping an investor judge the business acumen of the REIT manager and whether they have overpaid for a certain acquisition or if they have gotten a good deal for shareholders.

Intuitively, an attractive REIT is one that derives good cash flows from the quality assets that it owns. Thus, the cap rate essentially tries to capture how attractive the property is in terms of the yield. Needless to say, the NPI used in the calculation should represent a stabilized income for the property for that time period to get a stabilized and realistic cap rate.

In Capitaland Mall Trust Full Year 2019 Financial Results, the Valuations and Valuations Cap Rates table detailed the Cap Rates of its various properties at end-2019, as well as the valuation at end-2019 and the variance from the last valuation. A closer study revealed information such as:

a.   Suburban malls, which have been very defensive in the past two decades, showed very tight cap rates of between 4.5% as in the case of Westgate in Jurong East to 4.8% as in the case of Bukit Panjang Plaza. The variability is only 30 basis points.

b.   Urban malls showed a wider variability of cap rates of between 4.4% as in the case of Plaza Singapura on Orchard Road to 5.2% as in the case of Bugis+ in the Bugis area. This is a reflection of downtown malls' less defensive nature as most of them have a higher reliance on tourist spending compared to the locals' necessities spending.

A good grasp of the cap rates of the various types of properties and over different periods of time is highly useful in appreciating and understanding the highly cyclical nature of cap rates and the factors that affect it. Many investors tend to compare cap rates to the government 10-year bond yield to get the cap rate spread which normally helps shape the margin of safety in investing in certain properties.

In areas like Japan and Europe where the 10-year government bond yield is negative or near zero, acquiring properties that have cap rates of only 4+ % is still considered attractive. A good example is Mapletree NAC acquisitions of its Japanese portfolio where the bulk of the properties have cap rates of only 4+ %, but are still attractive and even yield-accretive as the Japanese bond yield is near zero %.

In cases of acquisitions, a capitalization approach based on a sustainable net income on a fully leased basis, is normally used in conjunction with understanding the current passing rental income and other relevant expenses. The latter normally include applicable outgoings, operating expenses, property management expenses and property tax.

The resultant net income is then capitalized at a certain cap rate for the remaining tenure of the property to produce a core capital value. The cap rate thus reflects the nature, location and tenancy profile of the property together with current market investment criteria.

LESSON LEARNED

The cap rate is a good measurement of the relative attractiveness of one property compared to another in the same area or grade. It also gives an indication if a REIT manager has overpaid for a property or gotten a good deal.

DISCOUNTED CASH FLOW ANALYSIS (DCF)

Similar to the DDM (see DDM section) which is used in valuing a REIT based on certain assumptions, the DCF is normally used to value the REITs' properties. The DCF seeks to allow an investor or owner to make an assessment of the long-term return that is likely to be derived from a property with a combination of both rental and capital growth over an assumed investment horizon.

For example, to get an idea of a property's 10-year prospect, a DCF is done based on the property's cash flow over a 10-year period and an assumption is made on the sale value of the property at the commencement of the 11th year of the cash flow.

The smart and sharp REIT investor should understand that in undertaking such analysis, a wide range of assumptions have to be made including a target or pre-selected internal rate of return, rental growth, occupancies, sale price of the property at the end of the investment horizon, costs associated with the initial purchase as well as the associated costs at the disposal of the property.

The accuracy of such forecasts is highly dependent on perceived market conditions in the future, estimated tenancy and cash flow profile and the overall physical condition of the property in 10 years' time. Practically therefore, it is a highly difficult task and the room for deviation from the actual calculation will be wide.

Thus, the DCF, like the DDM should at best, be used by the investor as an estimate in the framework of BUY/SELL investment decisions, but should not form the frame in the framework as it is dependent on too many variables and too many future assumptions of such variables.

REPLACEMENT COST METHOD

The other valuation measures like yield-based approach, P/BV, DDM, Cap Rate and DCF approaches valuation from an income-generating perspective of the property. The replacement cost method approaches valuation from a replacement valuation perspective – it questions how much it would cost to build a similar property to the same specifications in a particular location.

If the replacement cost far exceeds the original cost of the property, it is a very good indication of possible under-valuation of the REIT price, especially if the price has not moved and vice versa. I am always on the lookout for properties like these which trade at below replacement cost over the years, a firm indicator that either the asset was bought cheaply originally or that management was able to buy the property before the market went up. This is key in making your millions in REITs!

I find the replacement cost method a very good counter-intuitive valuation method especially for new asset classes like cell towers, business parks, data centres, student lodging and timber assets. It is also highly useful in the traditional property sectors where transactions are few and far in between. Of course, the availability of reliable information needed to apply the Replacement Cost method is paramount.

Let me illustrate.

Date	Business Park	Estimated Floor Area (GFA/NLA)	Transacted Price	Price
3Q2017	13 Business Park	108,888	$24,800,000	$227.76
4Q2016	DSO National	848,959	$420,000,000	$494.72

	Laboratories 1&2			
	DNV GL Tech			
	Centre			
3Q2016	Mapletree	1,708,218	$1,780,000,000	$1,042.02
	Business City 1			
4Q2015	One @ Changi	679,267	$420,000,000	$618.31
	City			
1Q2015	The Kendall	181,291	$112,000,000	$617.79

Selected business park investment transactions since 2015

In the Mapletree Commercial Trust (MCT) Circular Dated 27 September 2019 on its proposed acquisition of Mapletree Business City II (MBC II) for $1.550 billion, there were only five business park transactions in the past five years from 2015 to 2019. Yes, an average of one per year.

What is also amazing was that historically, City Fringe business parks like MBC I and MBC II have commanded average rental premiums of 49.4% over the Rest of Island submarket since 2014. As of 2Q2019, the City Fringe and Rest of Island submarket commanded rents of $5.80 per square foot/month (psf/month) and $3.80 psf/month, respectively. In fact, from 2014 to 2019, business parks in the City Fringe have enjoyed a huge rental premium of 40% to 50% premium over the Rest of Island business parks. Thus, location and the asset quality of a business park are critical to nail down good rentals and yields.

Business parks, a relatively new sector for REITs in Singapore, have exhibited a two-tier market for almost a decade with the City Fringe vacancy rates approaching a low of 6.4% while the Rest of Island hit a high of 17.2% in 2Q2019.

The premium enjoyed by the City Fringe submarket is in fact driven by different profiles of tenants that typically occupy the City Fringe business parks, as well as relative proximity to the CBD. In addition, the buildings in the City Fringe business parks are generally newer, with higher premium technical specifications like large column-free floor plates, high floor-to-ceiling height and located in lush greenery environment spread over five hectares of land with Grade A office-like specifications.

MBC II has an NLA (Net Lettable Area) at 1,184,704 square feet comprising 1,167,106 sqft for the business park and 17,598 sqft for the mostly F&B retail area. The transaction thus worked out to $1,308.34 psf.

Many would balk at the high transaction cost on a per square foot basis if you had used the price achieved for 13 International Business Park which was transacted in 3Q2017 at just $228 per GFA. MBC II would have come across as almost 6x or 574% more expensive.

If one had used the valuation achieved for MBC I (since MBC I is on the same premises as MBC II) which was consummated in 3Q2016 at $1,042 per NLA in 3Q2016, then it would have indicated that MBC II cost 25.53% more in just three years! Thus, MBC II seemingly was being valued at a premium to MBC I (see the section below on Comparable Sales Method for a deeper elaboration).

The replacement cost method is certainly a good indicator of the current price of an asset. It certainly reflects how business parks, as a scarce asset class, has appreciated in the past three years. This would be different from the book value of an asset as the latter reflects the historic purchase price less accumulated depreciation.

LESSON LEARNED

The replacement cost method is a good counter-intuitive way of valuing new asset classes like business parks, data centres, student lodging and timber assets. It is also a good indicator of the current price of an asset where past transactions are scarce and/or not located in the same geographical area.

COMPARABLE SALES METHOD

The Comparable Sales method provides an observable value for a property acquisition against other recent transactions. It is one of the most widely used approaches as it is easy to use, to calculate and the data is most current. Moreover, most valuers are reluctant to make any large adjustments to valuations without transactional evidence.

Let's continue to illustrate using the MBC II acquisition.

In the Independent Advisor's Letter by Australia and New Zealand Banking Group Ltd, Singapore Branch (ANZ) on the MBC II acquisition, ANZ conceded that there was no perfect comparable to MBC II. Thus, they compared MBC II to Comparable Office Properties in terms of location, building specifications, tenant quality and remaining tenure to help assess the transaction price of $1,308 psf.

The valuation per Net Lettable Area (NLA) implied by the acquisition of $1,308 psf was the highest for the range of valuation per NLA of the business parks compared to. These included MBC I, Solaris, Neuros, Immunos, Nexus @one-north, Changi Business Park Collection, Science Park I collection and Science Park II collection. I find it quite strange that MBC II was compared to the other business parks like Changi Business Park.

Changi Business Park is a second-generation business park launched in 1997 in the east region whereas MBC II was completed in 2016 and located in the west region. Changi Business Park tenants' profile of DBS Bank, Honeywell, Xilinx, Huawei, Ericsson, Citi Group and EMC Computer Systems, just to name a few, are quite different from those at MBC II in terms of profile, the industries they operate in, etc.

MBC II's anchor tenant is Google which is the global web search engine. Google has expanded into a wide range of internet and technology related services, products and research and development which include specialized areas in artificial intelligence, cloud computing and software development. MBC II in fact houses Google's Asia Pacific HQ.

With Google as the main tenant, the technology sector constitutes 78.8% of the tenants profile of MBC II by trade mix, certainly very different from Changi Business Park or Science Park.

Using the comparable sales method, the past transactions of business parks worked out to $523 psf for Science Park II Collection at the low-end and $1,285 psf for MBC I at the high-end. It is noteworthy that MBC I valuation has increased from $1,042 psf based on the purchase price in 3Q2016 to $1,285 psf by 31 August 2019, the latest valuation then. This implies a 23.32% growth in value in just three years, which means that the acquisition price of $1,308 psf for MBC II is no longer expensive (as seemingly so in the previous section on Replacement Cost) and could be seen as attractive in view of MBC I's growth in the past three years since acquisition.

LESSON LEARNED

The Comparable Sales method provides a good observable value for a property acquisition against other recent transactions. It is one of the most widely used approaches as it is easy to use, to calculate and the data is most current. However, the sagacious REIT investor should always question if samples used in such comparison are indeed comparable and where possible, spot the essential differences with the other comparable properties.

Chapter 6

THE RISKS OF INVESTING IN REITS

REITs are traded on the stock exchange which means that they have risks similar to equity investments as well as risks emanating from the real estate sector that they are operating in. The experience of the S-REIT market has shown that REITs tend to trade more as investment equities that invest in real estate properties, rather than mirroring the real estate returns in the various sectors that the REITs invest in.

Compared to other investments such as equities, bonds, foreign currencies and commodities, REITs are subject to various risk factors that affect total returns. Although REITs' long-term returns have been impressive and have outperformed both bond and equity indices, there have been periods of underperformance, albeit for a short period of time.

REITs can be particularly unforgiving for investors who overlook their imbedded risks. This fact dawned upon me during the GFC of 2007 to 2009. Ever since, it has helped me look at REITs like an old song goes – *The Good, The Bad and The Ugly*. Firstly, to avoid the ugly, you must learn how ugly really looks like. In this chapter, we will study in detail the most overlooked risks of active REIT investing.

The other thing that underlies my REIT investment is that risks rear their head when they are least expected. Thus, I will end the chapter on Minimizing Your Risks to help ensure that you are always prepared as the smart REIT investor.

REFINANCING RISK
Borrowings are an integral part of REITs. REITs will almost always

need to borrow from banks while subject to the gearing limit of 45% (recently moved up to 50% because of COVID-19) as imposed by the Monetary Authority of Singapore (MAS). Thus, the gearing level of the REIT and how long or short its average debt maturity, will determine how often it needs to engage the debt market to refinance its debts.

Essentially, the lifeblood of a REIT is the ability and need to procure financing at reasonable costs and in the quantum needed. Thus, any wide fluctuations in debt markets, caused by crisis conditions like COVID-19, will severely impact the financing ability of a REIT or its cost of refinancing.

The need to use leverage also means that the REIT may need to incur additional expenses relating to additional fees incurred in connection with borrowings, in addition to interest payments payable on the loan amounts drawn. For the REIT shareholder, it is crucial to pick REITs that do not land you in a vulnerable position when the REITs resort to rights issues to raise capital during a crisis. A crisis is when prices of most, if not all REITs, are at the cheapest, but it can also be a time when investors are most strapped for cash.

For example, during the GFC in 2008, CapitaLand Mall Trust (CMT), then known as CapitaMall Trust, had to resort to a deeply discounted rights issue of 9 for 10 shares at $0.82 per share, a sharp 43.4% discount to the then market price of $1.45.

CMT had to resort to the rights issue as the CMBS loans market which was widely tapped on by REITs from 2005 to 2007, practically came to a standstill during the GFC as counter-party risks rose. Moreover, CMT became vulnerable as it had expanded too quickly and had allowed its gearing ratio to increase from 25–30% previously to 43.2% during the GFC, slightly below the 45% limit then. This meant that it had little choice and would have breached the 45% gearing limit if asset values continued to fall, without the rights issue. Note that REITs that resort to rights issues at sharp discounts without any commensurate asset purchases will lead to immediate dilution for shareholders as well as falling DPU in the next few quarters.

A gearing ratio or leverage ratio is the financial ratio that indicates the level of debt of the REIT against its other assets or against its equity in its balance sheet, income statement or cash flow statements. They are good indications of how the REIT's assets and business operations are financed.

The most widely used leverage ratios are:

a.   Debt-to-Asset Ratio = Total Debt/Total Assets

b.   Debt-to-Equity Ratio = Total Debt/Total Equity

c.   Debt-to-Capital Ratio = Total Debt/(Total Debt + Equity)

d.   Debt-to-EBITA Ratio = Total Debt/(Earnings before interest expense, taxes and amortization/depreciation)

Of course, in doing such a massive deeply discounted rights issue at a crisis time, shareholders that could not take up their pro-rata rights entitlement, had their stakes reduced significantly and subsequently were subject to a long period of lower DPU as the share base had increased.

Studies have shown that REITs with high debt-to-equity/asset ratios will have higher financial distress costs. During the subprime mortgage crisis in 2007 to 2009, real estate and REIT values declined substantially, forcing REITs with high debt-to-equity/asset ratios to divest assets at low prices and raise capital on stock markets at high cost in efforts to pay off interest expenses and loans that became due.

In Singapore, this resulted in two casualties – MacarthurCook Industrial REIT, which was listed in 2007, went into financial difficulties during the subprime mortgage crisis of 2007 to 2009. By early-2000, the REIT was bailed out by AMP Capital and other financial investors via successive recapitalizations and re-positioning of its asset portfolio. Minority shareholders who were unable to fork out additional capital to take part in the recapitalization exercises were immediately diluted. AMP Capital and AIMS Financial Group managed to secure control over the REIT manager eventually and renamed the REIT as AIMS AMP REIT.

The subprime mortgage crisis also claimed another REIT victim. On July 2008, it was announced that 17.7% of Allco Commercial REIT as well as its REIT manager would be sold to Singaporeconglomerate Fraser & Neave for $180 million. Allco was the unit of troubled Australian asset manager Allco Finance Group. The REIT was subsequently renamed as Frasers Commercial Trust which in turn was merged into Frasers Logistics & Commercial Trust in 2020.

During the COVID-19 Crisis, it was not surprising to see REITs with lower gearing ratios recover much faster than REITs which had flirted with the 40% gearing levels.

The MAS has proposed to raise the gearing limit (i.e. debt-to-asset ratio which is a measure of how well a REIT is capitalized) if REITs can demonstrate good interest coverage ratios (which is a measure of a REIT's ability to service its debt obligations from regular sources of income). It is unsure when and if, this new legislation will be passed.

Irrespective of the above outcome, we have always taught in our REITs investment classes that although leveraging as a financing method can result in higher dividend yields and attract REIT investors, they come at a greater price risk. Debt financing should only be implemented wisely to avoid higher price volatility as the REIT stands to lose investors who have low tolerance for higher credit and refinancing risks.

LESSON LEARNED

REIT managers who wish to raise capital though debt financing instead of equity should be cognizant of market timing. Unfortunately, not many S-REIT managers have been able to do that despite having armies of bankers to help them do just that. Ideally, debt should be drawn down when the cost of debt is low or during times when the cost of equity is high. Like many things in life, theory is always easier than practical, but this is where an investor can measure the calibre of a REIT manager most accurately.

INTEREST RATE RISK

Interest rate risks for REITs show up as Cost of Funds (COF) or financing costs. As REITs distribute a large portion of their income to unit holders with minimal retention to enjoy tax transparency, interest rate risk via higher refinancing costs is a perennial risk when loans mature. Obviously, if a REIT is unable to obtain refinancing and is required to sell off the property if they are mortgaged under the loan, the consequences on the REIT price can be tremendous as we saw in MacarthurCook REIT's case during the subprime mortgage crisis.

Over the years, the S-REITs that have exhibited lower COFs or financing costs tend to have either a strong sponsor, a good REIT manager or good quality of assets where banks are more comfortable to lend to and lend on or a combination of the above.

We have always taught in our investment classes that the COF is a good way of interpreting what the bankers of the REITs are conveying to investors. If a REIT continually suffers from high COF or financing costs, it is a high reflection of a combination of non-optimal sponsor, manager or quality of asset. High COF or financing cost makes further acquisitions more difficult as banking covenants are more demanding and suck away at precious cash. This becomes more important when interest rates are rising.

In the S-REIT market, most of the REITs that have a higher COF are those that have assets located overseas. Unfortunately, Sabana REIT sticks out like a sore thumb as although all its assets are local, its COF stands close to 4% even through 2019 when interest rates had been on a decline. Not surprisingly, it has decided to merge (although the structure of the deal was more like a sale) with ESR-REIT in July 2020, after years of share price underperformance.

And not surprisingly, pursuant to the merger with ESR-REIT, the enlarged entity will initiate a $460 million five-year term loan to refinance Sabana's total borrowings of $294 million, pay the upfront land premium of $58.6 million for the redevelopment of Sabana's largest asset, New Tech Park at Chuan Road. The all-in cost of the $460 million loan is only 2.5%, much cheaper than Sabana's own COF of 3.8% and even cheaper than ESR-REIT's own COF of 3.54%. This is another good execution master stroke and a reflection of how good and astute the management team at ESR-REIT is. Moreover, the loan is of an unsecured nature. On a pro forma basis, this is expected to translate into savings of about $7.9 million. Interest expense savings is definitely a prime reason for many REITs looking to merge to get bigger and more profitable, very evident in the impending ESR-Sabana REIT merger.

In contrast, some of the best-performing REITs like Parkway Life REIT and Keppel DC REIT have low COF at below 2%. As Parkway Life REIT has been able to borrow in low-cost Japanese Yen to match its assets its Japan, it has been able to enjoy COF at below 1%. Ascott REIT, which is in the more cyclical hospitality business, has been able to perform much better against its peers as its COF is the lowest in the sector, partly attributed to its strong parentage – it is part of the CapitaLand Group. As a comparison, its latest COF at 1.8% on 31 March 2020 is less than half of ARA US Hospitality Trust's COF at 3.9%.

COST OF DEBT						
	31-Dec-18	31-Mar-19	30-Jun-19	30-Sep-19	31-Dec-19	31-Mar-20
Parkway Life REIT	0.97%	0.91%	0.91%	0.81%	0.80%	0.63%
Keppel DC REIT	2.20%	2.10%	1.70%	1.70%	1.70%	1.70%
Ascott REIT	2.30%	2.10%	2.10%	2.10%	2.00%	1.80%

Selected REITs with low COFs

There have been many instances where interest rate risks have been overlooked by investors, resulting in significant capital and DPU loss for shareholders. In our investment classes, we specifically spend a lot of time doing scenario analysis and prepare for various possibilities of REITs' financial and operating metrics to pre-empt financial deterioration in REITs because when high financing costs finally come home to roost, the share price can just head south very quickly. The more one studies the different REITs in the different sectors and geographical locations, the more an investor will understand that risks are indeed unique and non-uniform. And one must prepare and protect your REIT's portfolio from refinancing risk vulnerabilities.

> **LESSON LEARNED**
>
> Interest rate risks for REITs show up as Cost of Funds (COF) or financing costs. As REITs distribute a large portion of their income to unit holders with minimal retention to enjoy tax transparency, interest rate risk via higher refinancing costs is a perennial risk when loans mature. There have been many instances where interest rate risks have been overlooked by investors, resulting in significant capital and DPU loss for shareholders. The perspicacious REIT investor must always seek to prepare and protect against refinancing risks of his/her REITs portfolio.

EXCESSIVE RELIANCE ON CAPITAL MARKETS

Many investors love the stability and frequency of REITs' dividends or DPU. This allows the shareholders control over free cash flow, earn steady and growing dividends and minimize re-investment risk. REITs are able to deliver this love as they are mandated by law to pay at least 90% of taxable income as dividends for tax transparency. This would normally leave little cash buffer for the REITs.

The little cash buffer may force the REIT manager to tap external capital markets if and when it needs to make huge acquisitions. This is not negative per se as it allows minority shareholders to constantly review a REIT's acquisitions which effectively adds another layer of scrutiny. Theoretically, if an acquisition is going to be doubtful with minimal accretion to DPU or NAV and minimal positive impact on the overall portfolio, then it could be difficult to win shareholders' approval.

However, practically, if a REIT manager chooses to expand aggressively, then it inevitably becomes excessively reliant on the capital markets. Most REIT managers, not surprisingly, will not admit to this over reliance.

Case Study of Manulife REIT

On Tuesday, 24 March 2020, at the climax of the COVID-19 crisis sell-down, the local media reported that "the manager for Manulife US REIT blamed the REIT's horrific price drop, which wiped out four years of work, on mass selling by index funds and exchange traded funds, margin calls from private banks, and funds redemption and switching to other counters amid rising volatility due to the US COVID-19 situation."[1]

Manulife REIT was certainly one of the worst-10 performing REITs in the COVID-19 crisis sell-off, together with the other US-listed REITs like Keppel Oak Pacific REIT and Prime REIT. We had warned our student investors to AVOID these US REITs in our investment classes previously. Our high level of conviction to avoid Manulife REIT, which we had explained in detail in our classes included:

1. A lackadaisical growth in DPU despite more than 160% growth in AUM to US$2.1 billion at end-2019 compared to its IPO asset size of just US$799 million on 12 May 2016.

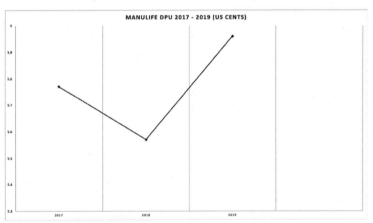

MANULIFE DPU 2017 - 2019 (US CENTS)

Manulife Manulife's lackadaisical growth in DPU despite a more than 160% growth in AUM to US$2.1 billion at end-2019

2. Manulife REIT's aggressive growth at the expense of its older properties, namely Figueroa and Michelson, both of which suffered lower NPI in FY2019. Even its newly-acquired The Exchange suffered negative NPI growth despite a strong office market in its 4Q2019 results.

3. Stripping out its newly-acquired properties from the original IPO property portfolio, it was clear that the original IPO properties were actually facing unexciting NPI growth.

---

1   *Business Times*, 24 March 2020.

4. Despite an aggressive acquisition strategy, NAV, like its DPU had not grown. Instead, it has sputtered at US$0.79 as at end-2019.

5. Despite the office rental market in the various areas where its assets were located having NIL deliveries, i.e. NIL supply growth, the rental growth of its various properties hardly seemed to reflect such a phenomenon.

6. Many investors have started to question if the acquisition strategy was related to its aim to enter the FTSE EPRA/NAREIT Index especially since the DPU had remained flat.

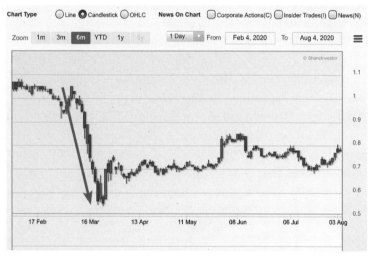

Manulife REIT suffered one of the largest sell-downs during the COVID-19 Crisis. Source: ShareInvestor.

The Sell-Down

In its teleconference call, Manulife REIT "tried to inspire confidence in the REIT by affirming that its leases are secure despite tenants working from home temporarily and some tenants downsizing. The REIT is nowhere near breaking any financial covenants either." (Please refer to footnote 1.)

Student investors at GCP Global who have been attending our REITs Quarterly Classes since 2010 will know that we have repeatedly warned about REITs that expand too fast in too short a period of time. Investors should be able to see if acquisitions bear fruit and the quality of the fruit first before REITs continue on their acquisition spree.

The REIT IPO at US$0.83 on 12 May 2016 with an asset under-management (AUM) of US$799 million comprising just three office assets in the US, namely the Figueroa, Michelson and Peachtree. By end-2019, it had expanded to nine properties valued at US$2.1 billion. Essentially, the REIT had tripled its number of properties from three to nine in just 3.5 years and the value of its AUM had almost tripled from US$799 million to US$2.1 billion over the corresponding period. However, in its latest FY2019 results, three out of nine Manulife properties have already exhibited a drop in NPI as compared to FY2018. This included its newly acquired The Exchange.

There is certainly nothing wrong for a REIT to expand via acquisitions after its IPO. However, investors would need to see the fruit of earlier expansions filtering down to the DPU they actually receive, first. Manulife had shown an adjusted DPU to reflect how the DPU had changed with each acquisition. However, investors pay special attention to the actual DPU, not adjusted DPU, as that is the dividend they receive. Too fast an expansion and too much fund raising in a short period of time may confuse investors, more so if the original assets in the IPO had started to show signs of growth plateauing.

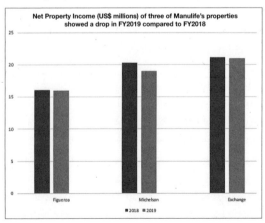

NPI of Figueroa, Michelson and The Exchange showed declines in FY2019 as compared to FY2018

Too Fast Too Soon?

Roughly a year into its IPO, Manulife REIT indicated that it wanted to double its AUM to US$1.6 billion. It then acquired The Plaza at Secaucus in New Jersey for US$116 million. In our classes, we noted that –

1. The acquisition was funded by a 41 for 100 deeply discounted rights at US$0.695 or a sharp discount of 28% to the closing price of US$0.965 per unit on the SGX on 31 August 2017, being the last trading day of the units prior to the announcement of the rights issue. The rights intended to raise US$208 million (S$283 million) from shareholders. Most REITs that undertake acquisitions, financed by rights issue at a substantial discount, will not do well at DPU growth. Over the decade, we have always emphasized that the most important factor in picking good REITs is their steady and consistent growth of DPU.[2]

2. Manulife initiated its quarterly reporting of Adjusted DPU. It then acquired 1750 Pennsylvania Avenue in Washington DC for US$182 million and Phipps Tower in Buckhead, Atlanta, in 2018 for US$205 million. These acquisitions increased its AUM by US$387 million to US$1,695.5 million in April 2018.

In May 2018, Manulife REIT had to raise funds again with another rights issue, this time it was a 22 for 100 rights at US$0.865 to raise US$198 million (S$265 million). The rights were at a sharp 7.9% discount to the VWAP of US$0.9391. Again, shareholders had to bear the burden of another heavily discounted rights issue to pay for the acquisitions.

We continued to highlight in our classes that –

a. These four acquisitions failed to raise DPU growth on a consistent and steady basis. Not surprisingly, Manulife REIT price continued to crawl through 2018, a reflection of its flattish DPU growth.

---

2   "The Ability to Deliver DPU Growth is the Key in SREITs Outperformance in 2018," *GCP Global*, 3/1/2019, https://gcpglobalsg.wixsite.com/gcpglobal/post/the-ability-to-deliver-dpu-growth-is-the-key-in-sreits-outperformance-in-2018.

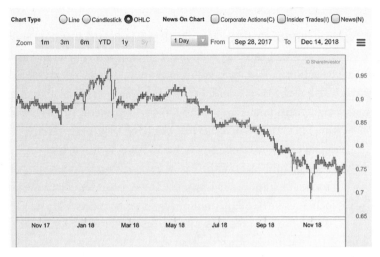

Manulife share price on a constant downtrend throughout 2018, a reflection of its flattish DPU growth despite active acquisitions. Source: ShareInvestor.

b.   Its Adjusted DPU interpretation caused confusion among investors as investors had to question and grapple in their crowded cerebellum if each quarter's DPU was adjusted for rights issue or with NPI from new asset acquisitions or a combination of such reasons. And for each of the reasons, how much was the DPU adjusted for and over which period of time. Which is which? Simplicity, not confusion is what investors seek for in REITs.

It then mentioned that it wanted to double its AUM to US$2.5 billion to be eligible to enter the FTSE EPRA/NAREIT Index.

Manulife REIT then went on to acquire The Centerpointe in Virginia, Washington for US$122 million in April 2019 and 400 Capitol in Sacramento, California for US$198.8 million in September 2019. This time round, both acquisitions were financed by private placements, at sharp discounts to the market price. It would not be a surprise if some of the "index funds and exchange traded funds" and institutions which the manager alluded to, in the sell-down in March 2020, bought into the placements then.

REIT managers can and should exercise discretion in who they can place out their shares to in a private placement. Maybe if the bulk of the placement shares were awarded to long-term funds or long-only institutional funds, the sell-down in the shares in March 2020 would not have been so severe? Perhaps Manulife REIT can take a leaf from newly-listed peer Prime REIT which declared that their private placement in February 2020 at US$0.957 was placed out to "long-only institutional investors, private wealth clients and multi-strategy funds". This will help avoid substantial sell-off in share prices during a crisis. It may sound nice to say that your REIT is backed by institutional investors, but do they really have your back in times of crisis?

Cheap Price is What You Pay in a Crisis, Value is What You Get

Manulife REIT's share price plunged to as low as US$ 0.555 as at Monday, 23 March 2020, a huge 46.64% drop. It was a historic low for Manulife REIT. In our classes, we have taught our investor students where and how to look for bargains in the market. Manulife REIT, despite its various shortcomings and our reservations highlighted above, would fit into the bargain zone at its recent low of US$ 0.555, as highlighted in our weekly Facebook Live sessions,[3] where we guided our student investors through the crisis.

Years of abstinence and patience are what the smart REIT investor endures in waiting to buy on the cheap. And crises are the best time to source for such REITs at a bargain.

There is nothing wrong with REITs' expansion per se, like Manulife's stated objective to double its AUM. However, the sagacious REIT investor must be cognizant that should for one reason or another, such REITs lose access to the capital markets, or suffer a spike in interest rates, however temporarily, their share prices would be in for a rout, as what Manulife REIT's share price went through during the COVID-19 crisis. Its share price crashed from $1.05 as at 19 February 2020 to an intra-day low of 54.5 cents on 23 March 2020. As at 30 June 2020, its share price hovers at 75.5cents, a substantial 28.10% below the pre-COVID-19 crisis levels.

3   https://www.facebook.com/gabrielyap17/videos/628938364620473/

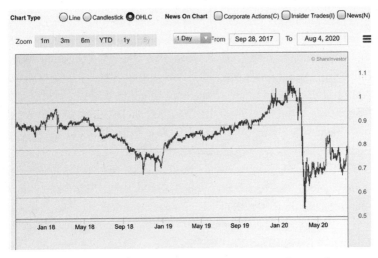

Manulife price since IPO. Share price practically gave back the gains, not once but twice, despite a more than 160% jump in AUM to US$2.1 billion since IPO. Source: ShareInvestor.

Many potentially disruptive developments affecting REITs are taking place with increasing frequency. What REIT managers should understand is that news, especially bad news, travels around the world almost instantaneously, no thanks to the ease of modern communications and the internet.

LESSON LEARNED

The upshot of this is that the value of a REIT can plunge severely, such as in Manulife REIT's case before there is a chance to clarify or react. That's why it is essential for REIT managers to keep a close watch on the myriad strategic, tactical, placement and potential risks that can impact them and the REIT price. Acquisitions for growth should not be rushed. Rather, the impact of past acquisitions on a REIT's DPU growth should be studied and understood by the smart and sharp REIT investor first. And a REIT cannot assume that all its expansion plans are clearly understood by investors in potentially disruptive times. The consequence will be on the share price.

INCOME RISK

The passing of the COVID-19 (Temporary Measures) Bill brought to the forefront Income Risk for REIT investors. The suspension of rent under the Bill can delay a REIT of its main source of income for up to six months. Potentially, a REIT also becomes susceptible to bad debts if the tenant is still unable to pay the rent after the suspension.

Not surprisingly thereafter, many REITs, particularly in the badly affected sectors like Retail and Hospitality, began holding back dividends in their 1Q2020 Results or 1Q2020 Business Update. As the REITs announced their results or updates, the retention of dividends came from various sources:

1.   Distribution Income
2.   Capital
3.   Non-payment of previous capital gains
4.   Retention from rentals received by a particular tenant
5.   Special Provisions

The extension of the period for the distribution of FY2020 taxable income from three months to one year will help REITs by giving them more time to manage their cash flows and work with tenants on their respective rental payments. Under the tax transparency treatment, a REIT is not taxed on income that is distributed to unit holders provided the payout is 90% or more.

REIT investors faced with the problem of lower DPU in the immediate quarters have to keep their fingers crossed that the deferred rentals owed to them will be paid in the future as the REIT needs to qualify for tax transparency. However, it is unclear what will happen if a tenant defers its rental under the Bill and after six months, its cash flow still does not improve and it even has to seek bankruptcy. The REIT's DPU will certainly be affected in such a scenario.

Dividends may not be paid if a REIT reports an operating loss or like what COVID-19 brought to roost – if tenants are allowed under temporary legislation, to defer their rental payments.

Income risk is also dependent on reversionary rentals being renewed at lower levels as vacancies rise. Investors should enquire if the REIT has taken mitigating measures like procuring a sufficient amount of security deposit, payment upfront or contractual lock-ins of rental rates and other clauses in tenancy agreements. COVID-19 certainly brought Income Risk to the forefront.

CONCENTRATION RISK

Concentration risk arises from either a geographical concentration of properties or tenant concentration. Investors would ideally want to see a portfolio of properties across multiple cities rather than a property in one micro-market making up a majority of the REIT assets.

Moreover, investors do not want a single tenant making up a vast chunk of the total rental income. Having a high tenant concentration means the loss of revenue and rental will be massive if the major tenant defaults. For instance, the impact of just two tenants, namely Technics Oil & Gas and NK Ingredients (Singapore) Pte Ltd, filing for judicial management, in consecutive years, had tremendous impact on Soilbuild REIT's fortunes and its share price performance.

A REIT with a good mix of tenants is less exposed to concentrated and idiosyncratic risks, especially towards risks of known unknown implications or of unknown unknown nature. In the same vein, it is interesting to note that newly listed Elite Commercial REIT only has one tenant – the UK government via The Secretary of State for Housing as its tenant. The REIT made its debut on SGX on 6 February 2020 at an IPO price of £0.68, the first-ever £ listing on SGX. The REIT suffered a sell-off to below £0.50 from the COVID-19 Pandemic and closed at £0.70 as at end-June 2020, barely €0.02 above its IPO price on very low volumes.

LIQUIDITY RISK

A change in the illiquidity of one asset class can affect a REIT's relative attractiveness. This was brought to the forefront during the GFC of 2007 to 2009. An illiquidity shock in one market can influence the demand for the asset and related assets in the same sector. Linkages across financial, capital and real estate assets can result in a flight-to-quality phenomenon during a crisis period. The reverse is true when markets calm down and experience a flight-from-quality as risk-on behaviour heightens.

REITs primarily invest in real estate markets, which are segmented. REITs with assets located in different markets should be subjected to different levels of illiquidity based on the markets where their properties are located.

Although REIT investors can buy or sell the REIT units fairly easily on the exchanges, the real estate in a REIT may be relatively less liquid or subject to government regulations of usage. This gives rise to liquidity risk for REITs as it can become difficult to quickly find buyers for property on short notice should there be any adverse economic conditions.

Soilbuild REIT's adventure or misadventure with its ownership of 72 Loyang Way is a classic case in point. This Industrial REIT was listed on the SGX on 16 August 2013 at an IPO price of $0.78.

Soilbuild Business Trust DPU peaked in FY2015 at 6.487 cents and has continued to decline through to 4.22 cents in FY2019. This is a sharp 35.95% decline over four years. We had forewarned our student investors way back in 2016 to AVOID the REIT as other than two exceptions in 3Q2015 and 4Q2016, the REIT has registered consecutive negative quarter-to-quarter DPU growth in the last 22 sets of quarterly results.

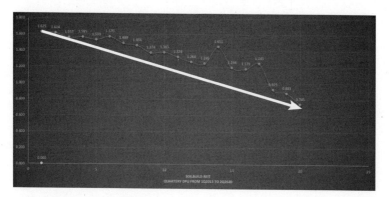

Soilbuild REIT has registered negative quarter-to-quarter DPU growth in the last 22 sets of quarterly results since 1Q2015

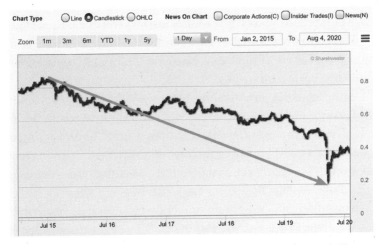

| Chart Type | ○ Line ◉ Candlestick ○ OHLC | News On Chart | ○ Corporate Actions(C) | ○ Insider Trades(I) | ○ News(N) |

| Zoom | 1m | 3m | 6m | YTD | 1y | 5y | 1 Day ▾ | From | Jan 2, 2015 | To | Aug 4, 2020 | ☰ |

Soilbuild REIT price from 2015 – the share price decline mirrors the steady decline in its DPU.
Source: ShareInvestor.

The REIT paid $97 million for the acquisition of a property at 72 Loyang Way on 27 May 2015. The acquisition-related costs amounted to an additional $1.12 million. In its factsheet dated 12 March 2015, it described 72 Loyang Way as offering a "rare and unique seafront property." The property is an integrated facility comprising two blocks of 3-storey and 4-storey ancillary office, two high-ceiling single-storey production facilities, a blasting and spray-painting chamber, a 200-worker dormitory and a jetty with 142 metres of sea frontage. In total, the property has an NLA of 171,293 square feet.

Trouble soon brewed for the REIT when its tenant, Technics Offshore Engineering Pte Ltd, defaulted on its rent within a year of its acquisition. The tenant operates in the offshore and marine sector which faced headwinds in the oil and gas sector in 2016. The tenant constituted 9.1% of rental payable at the time of default.

Upon default, the REIT faced an illiquidity problem in subletting out 72 Loyang Way as its shareholders realized that the property was subject to the Jurong Town Corporation (JTC) requirements to sublet to only tenants in the marine and offshore sector, which of course was facing the same headwinds as Technics. By 4Q2016, JTC temporarily lifted the subletting requirements on 30% of 72 Loyang

Way's gross floor area (GFA) to non-anchor tenants which may be operating outside the marine and oil sector. The key challenge was to find a qualified anchor tenant (which must be operating in the marine and oil and gas sector) to lease 70% of the property thereafter.

When it divested the facility on 21 March 2018, it only fetched $34.06 million, for a huge capital loss of $62.9 million or 64.86% over a time period of barely three years! It is certainly a staggering loss on the purchase price. Yet when the REIT reported the sale, it mentioned that the sale resulted in an estimated gain of $55,000. Of course, that "gain" was based on the revalued property value of $33 million based on the last valuation. Obviously, this meant that the property has been devalued down by as much as $64 million from its purchase price of $97 million. It is certainly anybody's guess if the original price paid of $97 million was astronomical or expensive.

REIT investors rely on managements to look after their investments, especially new purchases and disposals. A REIT will struggle to achieve sustainable growth if they overpay for assets which can be clearly seen in its declining DPU performance. Investors should always avoid REITs that undertake acquisitions with minimal margin of safety or capital recycling or new acquisitions with little benefits to shareholders. This would be evident from the share price performance following such actions. The market price of the REIT, following such acquisitions, is the best judge of the merits of such acquisitions.

Soilbuild REIT share price reached an all-time low of $0.1999 in the March 2020 sell-off. As of end-June 2020, the share price is at $0.39, down a woeful 50% from the IPO price of $0.78.

WORST PERFORMING REITS	IPO Date	IPO Price	30-Jun-20	Price Change	% Change
ARA US Hospitality REIT	9th May 2019	$0.88	$0.400	($0.480)	-54.55%
OUE Commercial REIT	27th Jan 2014	$0.80	$0.380	($0.420)	-52.50%
Soilbuilt Biz Trust	16th Aug 2013	$0.78	$0.390	($0.390)	-50.00%

Worst performing REITs (with trading history of less than seven years) as at 30 June 2020.

As a matter of comparison, not including Eagle Hospitality Trust which has been suspended, Soilbuild is one of the only three infamous S-REITs that are down by 50% or more from their IPO price based on a study of S-REITs with trading history of less than seven years. The other two REITs that have lost more than 50% from their IPO price are OUE Commercial REIT, down 52.50% and ARA US Hospitality Trust, down 54.55% as at 30 June 2020, compared to their respective IPO prices.

What the COVID-19 Crisis brought to the attention of REIT managers is that – you should understand that news, especially bad news, travels around the world almost instantaneously, no thanks to ease of modern communications and the internet. The upshot of this is that the value of a REIT can plunge severely, like in Soilbuild REIT's case during a crisis. This might have been prevented if the REIT's weak links were recognised and dealt with before the crisis mauled its share price. Investors expect REIT managers to implement and undertake effective asset and risk management by means of fruitful acquisitions that are yield-accretive, profitable divestments or undertake capital recycling opportunities that enhance the value of a REIT. The performance of the REIT price in the long term is a good indication of whether that has been achieved.

LESSON LEARNED

Although REIT investors can buy or sell the REIT units fairly easily on the exchanges, the real estate in a REIT may be relatively less liquid or subject to government regulations of usage. This gives rise to liquidity risk for REITs as it can become difficult to quickly find buyers for property on short notice should there be any adverse economic conditions.

Chapter 7

HOW REITS GROW AND HOW INVESTORS GROW WITH REITS

Most investors invest in REITs for a consistent and stable income. REITs pay out dividends or DPU on a quarterly or semi-annual basis. In the US, the most developed of REIT markets, some REITs even pay out dividends on a monthly basis.

In addition, investors seek to invest in REITs that strive to grow their DPU over time. The growth strategy of a REIT depends on the type of properties it owns and the lease structures of its underlying properties. An office REIT, which normally has leases for periods of 3 to 10 years would differ very much from a hospitality REIT where the Revenue Per Available Room (RevPAR) varies daily, each would have different strategies for growth and acquisitions.

In all these years, a proper understanding of the above will help investors choose the best-performing REITs. Broadly, REITs generate growth organically or inorganically.

ORGANIC GROWTH
Organic growth for REITs refers to growing the REIT's portfolio naturally. The three methods of organic growth are Rental Reversion, Asset Enhancement Initiatives (AEIs) and Capital Recycling.

Rental Reversion
Rental reversion increase is the most common way that a REIT grows its business organically. Rental income from tenants forms the majority of a REIT's business which simply is the collection of

such rentals, pay for normal operating expenses in operating the property and then paying out at least 90% of the income back to unit holders.

Naturally, investors should look for REITs with assets in operating markets that favour the landlord. In this respect, a close scrutiny and understanding of both present and future demand and supply conditions and the stage of the property sub-sector cycle is needed to pick outperforming REITs.

In the practical world of REITs, there are a few important factors that investors should be cognizant of:

a.   Some healthcare REITs and many US Office REITs have rental agreements with tenants that allow for annual escalations in their rental rates. For instance, Parkway Life REIT has an annual rental review mechanism that requires its sponsor, Parkway Singapore, to pay the higher of (base rent + variable rental of 3.8% of adjusted hospital revenue) for its three Singapore-based hospitals or the preceding year's rent + (CPI + 1%). Based on the above formula, Parkway Life REIT will still get a 1% increase in rental reversions even if CPI is zero. This rental formula makes Parkway Life REIT a very defensive REIT as it has been since its IPO in 2007. In fact, the REIT proudly plays up this point in its quarterly results where it says that it has "Downside Protection (By Gross Revenue) of 95%" on its existing lease agreements.

b.   Increasingly, REITs with foreign assets, like many REITs listed in Singapore with US assets, tend to have built-in rental increases for their base rentals upon renewals. For instance, newly-listed Prime US REIT came to IPO with 98% of its leases having embedded annual rental escalations of between 1% to 3% which supports future rental growth. The rental increases tend to be tied to an inflation index like the Consumer Price Index (CPI). Investors should always check that the former increases at a faster rate than the latter, rather than just be happy that their REITs have assets that run on leases that have gradual step-ups in annual rental rates.

c.   The definition of what constitutes rental reversion increases
      came into the spotlight three years ago when Keppel REIT
      redefined how it was calculating its rental reversion. Keppel
      REIT's definition of a rental reversion is:

$$\frac{(\text{Average Rent of New Lease Period})}{(\text{Average Rent of Expiring Lease Period})}$$

These rental contracts take into account:
i.   Renewal leases
ii.   New leases
iii. Forward renewal leases
iv.   Review leases

Not all REITs have the same interpretation or calculation of
Rental Renewal as the above formula, even within the same sector.
For instance, calculation of Rental Renewals at CapitaLand Mall
Trust and ESR-REIT are based on (New first-year Rent)/(Last
Payable Rent) and incorporated renewal rentals, new rentals and
forward renewal rentals.

     Ascendas REIT also uses the same formula, but takes into
account renewal and forward renewal rentals only. It does not
take into account new rentals. Thus, the smart REIT investor
should be cognizant of the different ways of calculating rental
reversions, the main staple of calculating a REIT's income.

d.   Different industries have different rental lease terms which
      reflect different industry practices and/or different geographical
      market conditions.

     The advantage of longer lease tenants is that they provide a
guaranteed stream of income for a longer period and the REIT
manager does not have to face the risk of sourcing for new tenants to
replace existing ones so regularly, especially in a down market.

     For instance, contrast the Weighted Average Lease Expiry (WALE)
for data centre REITs like Keppel DC at 8.9 years verses Lendlease

Global REIT's 313 Orchard asset which only has a WALE of 1.6 years at the point of its IPO on 2 October 2019.

The smart REIT investor should understand that a short WALE does not necessarily mean it is a higher-risk REIT. It could be the manager's conscientious decision to keep the WALE short so as to position the asset to benefit from rental upcycles especially when the sector demand/supply dynamics are about to shift upwards.

In the case of Lendlease, it was unfortunate that COVID-19 hit in January 2020, barely three months after its IPO, which resulted in many tenants in 313 Orchard needing to close as they were of "non-essential services". Outlook for new and renewal rentals seemed poor and not surprisingly, the share price of Lendlease took a bigger beating during the COVID-19 Crisis sell-off as compared to Keppel DC REIT. Was it a case of poor timing or just bad luck?

But of course, a more conservative REIT investor would prefer REITs or assets with longer WALEs. There is always a trade-off between longer WALEs for lower yields and vice versa.

LESSON LEARNED

Investors should hunt for REITs that can grow their portfolio naturally. The three methods of organic growth are Rental Reversion, Asset Enhancement Initiatives (AEIs) and Capital Recycling. Investors should look for REITs with assets in operating markets that favour the landlord. In this respect, a close scrutiny and understanding of both present and future demand and supply conditions and the stage of the property sub-sector cycle is needed to pick outperforming REITs.

Asset Enhancement Initiatives (AEIs)

AEIs are normally improvements or renovations done to a property. Most AEIs are undertaken to keep the property up to date with modern and improved designs or to reconfigure the property for other types of commercial uses. Many retail and industrial REITs have used AEIs to maximize the plot ratio or to enhance an industrial building into a high-specification building.

These are normally undertaken with the aim of achieving a higher yield per square foot and to upgrade the tenant mix. In some cases, the whole area where the existing assets sits, is totally revamped and given a new lease of life.

When buildings are newer after a major AEI, it is normally easier to attract quality tenants and achieve a higher rental reversion. Industrial REITs like Ascendas REIT and Mapletree Logistics Trust have almost continuous AEIs on a yearly basis. In keeping with changing consumer needs and specific area development, retail REITs like CapitaLand Mall Trust and Frasers Centrepoint Trust have also undertaken retail asset enhancements and AEIs on a constant basis. Common AEIs include upgrading of toilet facilities and children's playground to draw in the "play falls" or footfalls.

AEIs also create better internal efficiency by reducing management costs over the long run or optimizing building plot ratios.

In the earlier decade of Singapore REITs, most REITs like CapitaLand Mall Trust and Frasers Centrepoint Trust were able to achieve AEI returns of more than 10% on an Internal Rate of Return (IRR) basis from malls like Plaza Singapura, The Atrium, Junction 8, IMM, Northpoint City and Anchor Point. However, recent retail AEIs are only able to achieve single-digit returns due to continual increase in asset prices.

It is important for the smart REIT investor to distinguish a REIT's need to undertake an AEI to remain competitive, so as to prevent future declines in rental rates, compared to an AEI done to maximize its usage, and hence the rental earned.

For example, in the competitive office and hospitality industries, refurbishments to remain competitive and facelifts are very different from AEIs. The former is essentially capital expenditure while AEIs would create new net lettable area to earn additional income and earn an investment yield.

For example, Manulife REIT's 2019 announcement of AEI expenditure of US$20 million to upgrade lift lobbies are more refurbishments and facelifts, undertaken more to remain competitive to help the buildings achieve their reversionary rentals.

Manulife REIT's Figueroa property is undergoing AEI which includes lobby renovation, a cafe addition and exterior landscaping which will cost US$8 million. Its Exchange property is also undergoing AEI which includes lobby renovation, security/life safety system updates and a new glass wall feature. The renovation will cost US$12 million.

Asset enhancement can unlock the hidden potential of existing properties and can be key drivers for business growth over the years. They can even enhance the overall value of the property.

AIMS APAC REIT (AA REIT) is certainly one REIT in the industrial sector that has undertaken the highest proportion of AEIs within its portfolio. As of 31 December 2019, they own 25 industrial buildings in Singapore. Since 2014, they have completed AEIs in seven of their buildings and have two more undergoing AEIs in 2020.

AA REIT's new asset acquisitions have been few and far in between compared to its relentless AEI efforts on its existing assets. Its first major overseas acquisition was six years ago when it acquired a 49% stake in Optus Centre, a business park located at Macquarie Park in Sydney for A$184.4 million (S$215 million then). Then on 15 May 2019, it acquired Boardriders Asia Pacific Headquarters in Burleigh Heads, Queensland, Australia for A$41.5 million (S$39.84 million then).

20 Gul Way is AA REIT's largest development project to date. The property comprises a five-storey ramp-up warehouse and logistics facility, incorporated into two buildings providing warehouse, logistics and ancillary office accommodation with a substantial hardstand marshalling yard.

The three-and-a-half-year project was completed in four phases, capitalized on increasing its plot ratio from 0.46 to 1.4 for Phases One and Two, and to 2.0 plot ratio for Phase Two extension and Three. The whole development increased the site's total floor area from 378,064 square feet to 1,656,485 square feet, nearly 4x the original size.

AA REIT share price in the past 5 years. Source: ShareInvestor.

However, the share price performance of AA REIT tells a different story. The share price of AA REIT has range-trade in a very tight zone of $1.32 to $1.48 in the past five years before the recent collapse to under $1 due to the COVID-19 crisis. From AA REIT's example, it seems that investors are not attracted to REITs that constantly undertake AEIs. REIT investors prefer REITs which have displayed a remarkable record of achieving outstanding positive-accretive returns from acquisitions.

> **LESSON LEARNED**
>
> It is important for the smart REIT investor to distinguish a REIT's need to undertake AEI from one of maximizing its usage which helps to maximize the rental earned. Refurbishments undertaken by REITs to remain competitive and facelifts are not the same as AEIs. The former are essentially capital expenditures while AEIs would create new net lettable area to earn additional income and earn an investment yield. Asset enhancement can unlock the hidden potential of existing properties and can be key drivers for business growth in the future.

Capital Recycling

S-REITs are increasingly focused on capital recycling programs, selling off non-core properties and using the proceeds to purchase new assets that improve the quality of their overall portfolio or to undertake AEIs. In fact, S-REITs accounted for just under 50% of all market transactions in the real estate sector since the past decade, and that figure is still increasing. Improving a REIT portfolio is often cited by REIT managers for undertaking capital recycling, but it can actually mean different things based on the property sector.

REIT management teams are taking a much more active role in managing their portfolios through more active acquisitions and dispositions. In fact, one of the takeaways from the GFC and the COVID-19 Pandemic was that higher quality assets tend to withstand difficult economic conditions better than lower quality assets. During credit crunches, banks tend to prioritize capital for the best assets and REITs with lower quality assets are not going to get the best value in terms of Loan-to-Value lending limit, loan rates and loan covenants when it comes to loan renewals or new lending.

Capital recycling entails selling underperforming assets and channelling funds into assets with stronger yields or better quality. Practically, it can be quite challenging. Nonetheless, this separates the sheep from the goats in the REIT manager sphere. For investors, how a REIT manager navigates capital recycling is a good indication of how good (no REIT manager has said they are bad anyway) and astute they are. Ideally, what investors want is for the REIT to achieve quality upgrade and enhance the long-term growth while being mindful of the cost of capital, leverage and capital market issues like direction of interest rates. This is often easier said than done and very few REIT managers have been able to achieve this level of capability, despite being backed by an army of bankers and advisors who are supposedly more in-tune with the fluidity of financial market conditions.

First, the REIT must decide what to sell. Most REITs would like to sell their "worst" properties. However, the "worst" properties could have the most potential for DPU and earnings dilution as the cap rates are normally the highest, making the yield very difficult to replace. Moreover, the "worst" properties could face huge pricing gaps between buyers' bid price and sellers' expectations, making the time to sell longer than normal, especially when markets are in more volatile conditions.

On the other hand, selling the "best" properties may mean missing out on the best long-term growth potential. The "best" properties also tend to have the best de-risking feature in the property portfolio. An additional factor to consider is the tax factor, as the sale of properties with high embedded capital gains can create onerous tax burdens in jurisdictions that have capital gains tax. Therein, lies the challenge for capital recycling.

REITs generally have a tendency to cling on to their assets, regardless of quality due to the continuity of the NPI that they provide. Understandably, recycling programs are easy to announce, but practically, it is harder to implement because when a REIT sells assets, they lose near-term income. So, unless they can replace the assets quickly, the NPI, Distributable Income and DPU are going to take a hit.

REITs will also engage in capital recycling to exploit opportunities in a new geographical area.

Asia's largest REIT, Link REIT which is listed in Hong Kong first expanded into Tier-1 cities in China with a RMB2.5 billion (S$555 million then) acquisition of EC Mall in Beijing in March 2015. The mall is located in Zhongguancun which is known as the "Silicon Valley of China" in the Haidian District that is mostly populated by young professionals and the middle class.

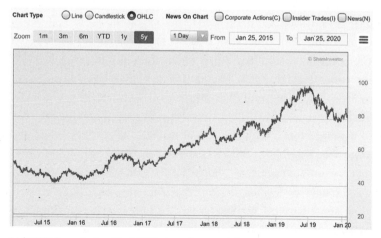

Link REIT share price since March 2015 when it first expanded into Tier-1 cities in China. Source: ShareInvestor.

It then followed quickly with the acquisition of Corporate Avenue 1 & 2 in Shanghai in July 2015. The property is a premium Grade A office with retail and car parks in the well-established Huaihai Middle Road CBD in Huangpu district.

Link REIT engaged HSBC, UBS and Cushman as advisors to assess strategic options for the REIT in July 2017. The study covered various growth options by referencing leading international REITs and property investment peers. It concluded that capital recycling remained the most efficient way to sustain growth trajectory for Link REIT. One of the plans mapped out was to expand into first-tier cities in China in a concerted way.

Subsequently, Link REIT disposed of a package of 17 properties with an aggregate appraisal value of HK$15.5 billion (S$2.621 billion then) at HK$23 billion (S$3.889 billion then) to Gaw Capital Partners for a disposal gain of HK$7.393 billion (S$1.25 billion then) on 28 February 2018. The deal for the 17-asset diversified retail portfolio as a bundle was unprecedented in terms of size and appeal to a broad array of investors. Some of the neighbourhood malls sold included H.A.N.D.S, Shek Lei and Kwai Shing East.

Less than nine months later, Link REIT utilized the proceeds to expand into Beijing, China with the acquisition of the Beijing Jingtong Roosevelt Plaza, a relatively new retail property in the Tongzhou district for RMB2.56 billion (S$512 million then).

As of the latest update of Link REIT in March 2020, Mainland China assets constitute 12.3% of its portfolio mix. Its portfolio value currently stands at HK$224 billion (S$40.8 billion).

REITs do dispose of their properties if they see limited growth, unfavourable supply/demand in certain geographies or to raise cash to acquire more profitable and/or younger properties or acquire properties with better WALE characteristics or to switch from over reliance on single tenant properties to properties that are more multi-tenanted.

A good sense of marketing, timing and/or luck is required to benefit from capital recycling. However, repeated good sense of market timing and/or luck can hint at astute management reading of markets. This is what the sharp and smart REIT investor should be looking out for.

For instance, Ascendas REIT sold its China asset, namely Ascendas Z-link for RMB760 million or S$160 million in 2016. It had bought it for only S$62 million just a little more than three years ago. To be able to make almost a 160% gain in just over three years speaks volumes for the shrewd buy that the REIT manager made. Ascendas REIT subsequently recycled the funds to Australia with a maiden portfolio purchase of 26 logistics assets worth A$1.013 billion on 18 September 2015. The share price of Ascendas REIT was then $2.20 when we first highlighted the stock to our student investors in our REITS Quarterly classes, Meet Ups and symposiums.[1]

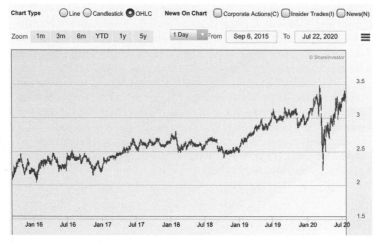

Ascendas REIT share price since 18 September 2015. Source: ShareInvestor.

Ascendas REIT subsequently replicated this geographical expansion, funded partly by capital recycling from sales of non-core assets into Europe and the US in 2019. Its share price reached $3.17 at end-June 2020, up $0.97 or 44.10% from its first maiden geographical expansion into Australia in 18 September 2015.

In essence, the REIT manager of Ascendas REIT was able to demonstrate the ability to increase asset quality, diversify geographic

---

1   GCP Global events, https://gcpglobalsg.wixsite.com/gcpglobal/gcpevents

exposure, lower balance sheet risk and lock in tremendous capital gain, all done with delicate and timely balance. This is what the perspicacious REIT investor should be looking out for and this is what makes Ascendas REIT one of our favourite stocks for the past two decades.

Investors should nevertheless take note that if the cash proceeds are not recycled into purchasing new properties, the DPU for the next financial year may drop from the lack of contribution from the sold asset. It is indeed a balancing act, but if executed well, is one of the best ways to judge how good a REIT manager is.

LESSON LEARNED

Capital recycling entails selling underperforming assets and channelling funds into assets with stronger yields or better quality. Practically, it can be quite challenging. Nonetheless, this separates the sheep from the goats in the REIT manager sphere. For investors, how a REIT manager navigates capital recycling is a good indication of how good (no REIT manager has said they are bad, anyway) and astute they are. Ideally, what investors want is for the REIT to achieve quality upgrade and enhance long-term growth while being mindful of the cost of capital, leverage and capital market issues like direction of interest rates. The ability of Ascendas REIT to execute its expansion into Australia, Europe and US, via expansion and capital recycling, is a good case in point. And the performance of its share price is a good testimonial.

INORGANIC GROWTH

Acquisitions

Acquisitions are undertaken by REITs to achieve scale effects as well as to deepen and/or diversify the income streams. Thereby, positive wealth effects for shareholders can be achieved. Positive economies of scale can be achieved by large REITs through size efficiency. This can be achieved from lower cost of capital, branding image, higher bargaining power with suppliers and tenants. However, the verdict is still out as to what constitutes critical size because size efficiency can diminish when the span of control of a REIT is exceeded.

There is strong evidence to suggest that the yield-accretive narrative propagated by most REITs in undertaking an acquisition is welcome by investors. Capital markets as well as shareholders look forward to higher revenue and higher NPI to translate into higher DPU.

Apparently, investors value growth stories for REITS, even though the key attributes of REITs as an investment vehicle are regular, stable and consistent dividend growth with minimal risk. Empirical evidence in the past two decades has now revealed that shareholders benefit when responsible REIT managers engage in property acquisitions that lead to higher earnings.

As this has been a key competitive advantage and key trait of picking outperforming REITs, we have dedicated a full chapter to assessing REIT acquisitions in detail: Chapter 8 – How to Analyse REIT Acquisitions.

Greenfield or Brownfield Development

REITs in Singapore can undertake property development utilising up to 10% of its property value in greenfield or brownfield development whereas J-REITs and HK-REITs are restricted from such riskier greenfield or brownfield development of assets or buildings on previously undeveloped land.

Greenfield development is seldom undertaken by S-REITs as the business of property development is often left to the parent and/ or sponsor who are usually big property developers. Of course, the developed property is often sold to the REIT thereafter.

There are pros and cons of REITs participating in greenfield developments.

One key advantage is that the REIT gets a toe-in into the future property at a cheaper entry price. This would be favourable for REITs with high cash balance and low gearing ratios at times when property valuations are at the high-end on the expensive side and almost all organic means of growth have been exhausted.

However, the disadvantages range from the higher risk profile of such projects and a long waiting time of three to five years before the property can start to generate income for the investors. Also, the REIT may have to source for a piece of land, undertake the construction and incur costs on borrowings via debt or lower payout to shareholders and to service interest costs on loans during the developing stage.

An example of a greenfield development is Ascott Residence Trust. It spent $62.4 million to acquire a prime greenfield site on 20 September 2018 for its maiden development project. It will build the first co-living property in Singapore's research and innovation business hub at one-north. It will be named lyf one-north Singapore.

It has commenced work on the project with 324 units. The entire project is estimated to cost $117 million and is expected to be fully funded by debt. lyf one-north Singapore development will account for about 3% of the REIT's total asset value, which is within the 10% regulatory limit on property development for REITs. The gearing ratio is expected to increase to 37.2% thereafter. The property is expected to welcome its first tenant only in 2021 and shareholders can only realize their DPU enhancement from the project then.

One of the reasons cited for undertaking the development is to build Ascott Residence Trust's pipeline of quality yield-accretive assets in Singapore, a mature hospitality market with stable performance at a time when it is becoming harder to find immediately accretive assets.

LESSON LEARNED

Strong empirical evidence in the S-REIT sector has shown that yield-accretive narratives propagated by most REITs in undertaking an acquisition and greenfield development are welcome by investors and the capital markets as shareholders look forward to higher revenue and higher NPI to translate into higher DPU.

Apparently, investors value growth stories for REITS, even though the key attributes of REITs as an investment vehicle are regular, stable and consistent dividend growth with minimal risk. Empirical evidence in the S-REIT experience in the past two decades shows that shareholders benefit when responsible REIT managers engage in property acquisitions that lead to higher earnings.

2 Development of lyf one-north Singapore

Purpose-built coliving property to appeal to the future traveller tribe

Coliving a rising trend in today's sharing economy amongst the **rising millennial-minded business traveller market**

lyf one-north Singapore, expected to **open in 2021**, incorporates 324 efficiently designed studio and loft units[1] and social spaces

one-north: **prime district** with **limited lodging supply** and home to **400 companies, 800 startups and 50,000 professionals**[2]

Attracting **over S$7 billion worth of investments**[2] and to be developed into a cluster of world class facilities and business parks

Notes:
1.   Subject to change
2.   Source: JTC (2018)

Ascott Residence Trust's maiden greenfield project, lyf one-north

Chapter 8

HOW TO ANALYSE REIT ACQUISITIONS

Acquisitions have been increasingly used by S-REITs to grow their asset size, earnings base and extend their geographical presence. S-REITs have taken advantage of low interest rates and set new records on asset acquisitions of $9.06 billion in 2018 followed by $10.24 billion in 2019. The staggering total amount of asset acquisitions of $19.30 billion in just two years is the highest ever recorded by S-REITs in any two years, since the S-REIT market commenced in 2002.

In any REIT acquisition deal, REIT managers have dual obligations. They should make sure that they are able to show and convince shareholders that the acquisition is a positive net present value investment and at the same time, demonstrate that the acquisition is consistent with the REIT's growth strategy.

Thus, it is very important for the smart REIT investor to fully understand the nature and quality of the assets being acquired, the domicile of the assets and the way the REIT finances the acquisition. REIT managers seek to justify every acquisition as "yield-accretive", but in essence, is this a sufficient criterion with which to assess an acquisition? Or are there other varied considerations involved?[1]

There is a huge difference between acquiring an asset at market price, which you and I can do, and getting a good deal for investors. Unfortunately, many REITs have done more of the former than the latter, with serious consequences to their REIT price. This chapter is designed to provide investors with a deep understanding of the nature of assets being acquired, the domicile of such assets and the way the REIT finances such asset acquisitions. Again, I have gained various

---

1   "Not all SREIT acquisitions have been wise and beneficial to minority shareholders", https://gcpglobalsg.wixsite.com/gcpglobal/post/not-all-sreit-acquisitons-have-been-wise-and-beneficial-to-minority-shareholders

GCP Global student investors gain first-hand knowledge and input from REIT CEOs or their respective heads of investor relations at our exclusive Investors Meet.

inputs in my personal encounters with the CEOs of REITs or their respective heads of investor relations in going through some of their deals as we meet these REITs every other month, doing our continued update and due diligence.

When used in good combination with sufficient market knowledge and experience, the investor will be able to unearth significant insights that separate the wheat from the chaff among the REITs. The smart investor will get a good perspective of profitability, financial flexibility, dividend safety, management capability, and long-term prospects of the REITs.

In the practical world, the smart investor should also understand that good and highly-accretive acquisitions are usually hard to come by during bullish market conditions. They normally coincide with easy-money market conditions when interest rates are low, but asset prices are relatively high. In contrast, during cyclically-down market conditions, there may be many bargain-buys, but financing may be expensive and interest rates are high.

REIT ACQUISITIONS IN 2019

Acquisitions by REITS in 2019 continued to be fast and furious, building on the momentum from 2018. April 2018 went down in the history of S-REITS as the month with the largest number of acquisitions announced. Five REITs, namely Manulife, Mapletree

Logistics Trust (MLT), Frasers Logistics Trust (FLT), Mapletree Industrial Trust (MIT) and SPH REIT all announced acquisitions totaling a whopping $1,368.36 million in a single month!

This record was subsequently broken in July 2019 when three REITs, namely Suntec REIT, Frasers Logistics Trust and CapitaLand Commercial Trust announced acquisitions that totaled $1,424.04 million.

S-REITS went on a rampage in 2019 with $10.24 billion worth of acquisitions. This was indeed an astounding new record! Coupled with $6.02 billion of new funds raised to finance the acquisitions, this record has taken on a new spin.

Understandably, due to limited investible local assets, S-REITs have been increasingly looking overseas for growth via acquisitions. However, growth via overseas acquisitions does not necessarily equate to growth in REIT prices for REIT holders as overseas acquisitions should be analyzed with greater scrutiny due to limited information and lack of independent avenues for verification of certain trends and facts in relation to reversionary rentals, occupancies and tenants' veracity and profile. In addition, the scare that emanated in 2018 from the tax transparency issue for REITs with US assets were real risks that smart REIT investors should take into account when evaluating REITs with overseas assets.

Most reports by analysts are based on the presentation materials dished out by the REITs, which naturally, will have to publish positive information to justify their acquisitions. The smart investor should always question if some of the information dished out to justify the acquisitions are indeed verifiable to justify the price paid.

LESSON LEARNED

Growth via overseas acquisitions does not necessarily equate to growth in REIT prices for REIT holders as overseas acquisitions should be analyzed with greater scrutiny due to limited information and lack of independent avenues for verification of certain trends and facts in relation to reversionary rentals, occupancies and tenants' veracity. The smart investor should always question if indeed some of the information dished out to justify the acquisitions are indeed verifiable to justify the price paid.

Acquisitions consummated in the past two years are indeed illuminating as S-REITs which became too adventurous in their foreign acquisitions saw their share prices underperform, in part due to an overhang of funds raised to finance such acquisitions as well as the market's scepticism towards such acquisitions. On the contrary, the REITs that executed good or even great acquisitions, performed well. These are the kind of REITs that the smart REIT investor should seek for.[2]

CASE STUDY OF GOOD REIT ACQUISITIONS – KEPPEL DC REIT

Throughout our investment classes, we have advised our students to have a strong positioning in Keppel DC REIT, Singapore's first-ever data centre REIT. Keppel DC REIT listed on 12 December 2014 at $0.93 with eight assets in six countries.

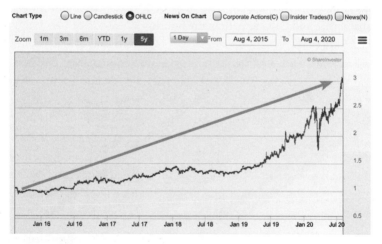

Keppel DC REIT share price has more than doubled since we recommended it in our REITs Quarterly class on Saturday, 13 August 2016. Source: ShareInvestor.

We have always advocated that S-REITs that can consistently make DPU-accretive acquisitions and employ shareholder-friendly financing structures to finance such acquisitions will be winners in the REIT sector. Such REITs will help enhance total return to unitholders

2   "Dealing with Volatility in the Year of the Rooster", *The Sunday Times*, 22 January 2017.

and increase the potential for future growth of the property portfolio through their astute acquisitions.

Keppel DC REIT made its second acquisition after its IPO on 12 August 2016 with the acquisition of the shell and core Milan Data Centre, its first Italian investment for €37.3 million. The acquisition enhanced the REIT's income stream stability with a 12-year double net-lease that included rental escalations and a six-year renewal option. The Milan Data Centre was fully-leased to one of the world's largest telecommunications companies and that acquisition extended its portfolio Weighted Average Lease Expiry (WALE), from 8.7 years then to 9.3 years.

We told our students who attended our Saturday, 13 August 2016 REITs class that this acquisition could mark a turning point for Keppel DC REIT (then priced at $1.14) since its IPO as the structure of the lease, the lengthened WALE, the relatively good price paid and the good quality of asset were the kind of attributes that would propel share price and DPU growth in the future.

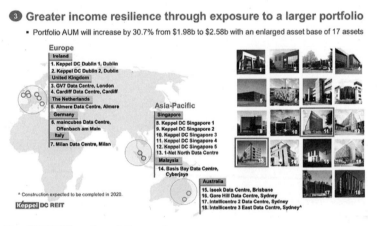

Keppel DC REIT's steady acquisitions over the years.

Data centre demand growth is forecast to take off, far outpacing supply growth as governments globally are planning to speed up broadband roll-out and boost e-commerce. Moreover, many of the technology majors are increasing information and technology outsourcing, cloud adoption and data sovereignty regulations that will drive data centre requirements.

Then barely two months later on 6 October 2016, Keppel DC REIT made another acquisition of a shell and core in Cardiff which was again fully leased to one of the largest global cloud service providers on a 15-year triple-net lease basis for £34.0 million. The new acquisition extended WALE further to 9.5 years and shared many of the merits of the previous acquisition.

This was another great acquisition as data centre users were looking to increase domestic presence or distribute data centres throughout the UK for broader coverage in the run-up to Brexit. Demand growth is forecasted to take off, far outpacing supply growth as the Internet of Things gains prevalence in the UK with significant investments in new technologies. Furthermore, the divergence of UK and EU data residency and compliance requirements following Brexit could increase the onshoring of data in both UK and Wales.

KEPPEL DC REIT		
Key Dates	Price	Event
12 Dec 2014	$0.93	IPO
12 Aug 2016	$1.14	Acquisition of 1st foreign DC in Mian
13 Aug 2016	$1.14	GCP Global Quarterly REITs class where we recommended a Strong BUY
6 Oct 2016	$1.16	Acquisition of data centre in Cardiff, Wales
17 Oct 2016	$1.18	Preferential Offer of 274 shares for every 1,000 at $1.155 to raise $279.5 million
30 Dec 2016	$1.185	2016 year-end closing
29 Dec 2017	$1.43	2017 ear-end closing
31 Dec 2018	$1.35	2018 year-end closing
31 Dec 2019	$2.08	2019 year-end closing
30 Jun 2020	$2.55	2020 mid-year closing

Keppel DC REIT then went on to acquire another $300 million worth of assets in 2017, followed by another $500 million in 2018 and ended 2019 with another record $600 million of new acquisitions, thereby driving up the AUM to $2.58 billion, comprising 17 assets across eight countries. Characteristically, most of the acquisitions shared the same important hallmarks: solid lease agreements that protected unitholders, lengthened portfolio WALE, and were good quality assets acquired at reasonable good prices, i.e. without overpaying. All these factors are instrumental in achieving continued share price rise and sustained DPU growth.

Acquisitions in 2019

Notably, the latest acquisitions of Keppel DC Singapore 4 at $384.9 million and 1-Net North DC at $200.2 million on 16 September 2019 continued to affirm the value-enhancing acquisitions that Keppel DC had been embarking on since its IPO.

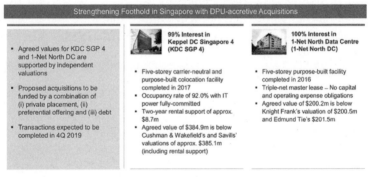

Keppel DC REIT's recent $384.9 million Singapore data centre acquisitions.

Its presentation slide (see below) showed the DPU enhancing impact of the acquisitions – they would boost DPU from 7.32 cents up to 8.01 cents; a whopping 12.4%, a far superior result to what other REITs had been achieving for their acquisitions in 2018 and 2019 which were in the less than 3% DPU impact range. This proposed impact was 400% or 4x more than the industry average!

> **LESSON LEARNED**
>
> The sharp and shrewd investor looks for REITs that make value-enhancing returns from the DPU accretion that new acquisitions bring. REITs that can deliver outsized DPU accretion from asset acquisitions will be the winners and outperformers.

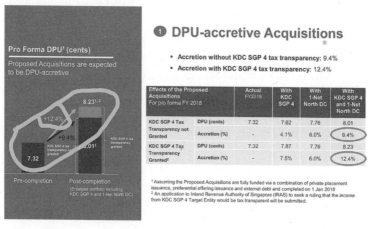

Keppel DC REIT's proposed DPU impact at 12.4% is a whopping 400% or 4x more than the industry average.

Financing Structure

Moreover, Keppel DC REIT's clever use of the financing structure to fund the acquisitions, enabled it to raise sufficient funds while securing the interest of existing shareholders. Funding comprised the following:

1. A private placement for 135 million shares @ $1.744 to raise $235.44 million at a mere 2.5% discount (compared to Cromwell REIT's private placement at €0.46 at a wide 11.7% discount to the VWAP of 0.5209 including married trades done on 20 June 2019 as highlighted in Chapter 4) to the VWAP of $1.7882

2. A preferential placement of 141.989 million shares @ $1.70 to raise $242.8 million, again at only a small discount of only 4.4% discount to the VWAP of $1.7882

Improving Existing Shareholders' Interests

In financing the acquisitions:

1. Existing shares were not diluted in a big way. The private placement discount of 2.5% was actually the joint-2nd best private placement done for 2019 at the least discount. The best was the 1.5% discount to VWAP of $2.4189 done by Frasers Centrepoint Trust on 16 May 2019 at $2.382 and the next best was the 2.5% discount to $1.539 executed by Ascendas India Trust on 19 November 2019 at $1.508.

2. Existing shareholders had a chance to participate in the preferential offer at $1.71 and to apply for excess rights shares. Of course, getting the excess rights was like striking lottery as the lowest prevailing price after 16 September 2019 was $1.80 and Keppel DC REIT went on to close at $2.08 at end-2019, a rare feat for S-REITs. The share price continued to rally in 2020 despite the COVID-19 crisis and it closed at $2.55 at 30 June 2020.

3. This was a highly DPU-accretive acquisition exercise that would enhance DPU by a whopping 12.4%, or 4x the industrial average. The smart and sharp REIT investor should compare this to Soilbuild Business REIT's acquisition of 25 Grenfell Street in Adelaide just a month earlier on 21 August 2019.

4. Soilbuild REIT went ahead with that acquisition despite the fact that the pro forma DPU impact would be negative – its Slide 23 of the presentation deck clearly stated that the acquisition would erode DPU by an astounding 3.3% from 4.98 cents to 4.82 cents if Scenario B was chosen. If the alternative Scenario A was chosen instead, the acquisition would still erode DPU by 1.4%, but it would send the REIT's gearing up to 39.7%, coming close to the 40% gearing level that many conservative REITs would avoid.

    Not surprisingly, Soilbuild REIT's share price went into a tailspin, falling from 58 cents on the date of announcement to as low as 48 cents in November 2019. It ended 2019 as the second-worst performing REIT, down to 52 cents or 11.54% on a year when all other REITs that had listed for more than a year, ended up in their share prices for 2019.

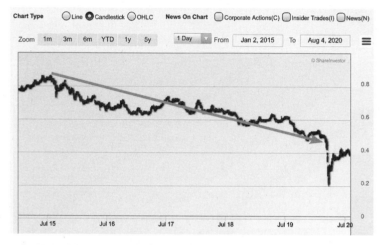

Soilbuild REIT's share price ended 2019 as the 2nd worst performing REIT, down 11.54% on a year when all REITs that had listed for more than a year, ended up. Source: ShareInvestor.

WORST 8 PERFORMING	Share Price	Share Price	Price	%
REITS FOR 2019	31/12/2019	31/012/2018	Change	Change
Eagle Hospitality Trust	$0.545	$0.780	-$0.235	-43.12%
Soilbuild REIT	$0.520	$0.580	-$0.060	-11.54%
ARA H Trust	$0.870	$0.880	-$0.010	-1.15%
First REIT	$0.995	$0.985	$0.010	1.01%
Frasers Hospitality Trust	$0.710	$0.700	$0.010	1.41%
Mapletree NAC	$1.160	$1.140	$0.020	1.72%
Cache Logistics	$0.715	$0.695	$0.020	2.80%
Suntec REIT	$1.840	$1.780	$0.060	3.26%

Worst 8 performing REITs for 2019

5. The financing structure Keppel DC REIT employed helped raise more than sufficient funds such that the REIT's gearing actually decreased from 31.9% to 30.3% after the acquisitions. This again, is another rare feat, among REITs. Compare this to

Soilbuild REIT's acquisition exercise which sent gearing up to the near-40% mark and the difference is even more stark.

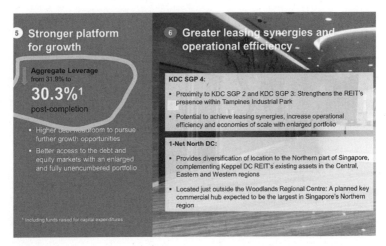

5 **Stronger platform for growth**

Aggregate Leverage
from 31.9% to

30.3%[1]

post-completion

- Higher debt headroom to pursue further growth opportunities
- Better access to the debt and equity markets with an enlarged and fully unencumbered portfolio

[1] Including funds raised for capital expenditures

6 **Greater leasing synergies and operational efficiency**

KDC SGP 4:
- Proximity to KDC SGP 2 and KDC SGP 3: Strengthens the REIT's presence within Tampines Industrial Park
- Potential to achieve leasing synergies, increase operational efficiency and economies of scale with enlarged portfolio

1-Net North DC:
- Provides diversification of location to the Northern part of Singapore, complementing Keppel DC REIT's existing assets in the Central, Eastern and Western regions
- Located just outside the Woodlands Regional Centre: A planned key commercial hub expected to be the largest in Singapore's Northern region

Keppel DC acquisitions of KDC SGP 4 and 1-Net North DC brought the gearing down to 30.5%.

Summary

In fact, the above are some of the attributes to judge whether REITs will perform well as acquisitions become in vogue going forward. In summary, the key benchmarks to judge whether a REIT has made good acquisitions are:

1. A fair or cheaper-than-market price paid for the asset
2. Whether the acquisition leads to a steady and longer WALE
3. The lease structure of the newly-acquired asset
4. The quality of tenants
5. DPU accretive impact
6. Yield accretive impact
7. NAV accretive impact
8. Financing structure to be advantageous to minority shareholders as placement shares were only on a slight discount to the VWAP and last done price
9. Financing structure to be advantageous to minority shareholders as they also get to participate in a rights issue at sufficient discount to the VWAP and last done price

Keppel DC REIT ended 2019 as the Best Performing REIT. Its capital gain was $0.73 or 54.07%. Including the total dividend of 7.61 cents for FY2019, the total return would have been much higher.

BEST PERFORMING	Share Price	Share Price	Price	%
REIT FOR 2019	31/12/2019	31/012/2018	Change	Change
Keppel DC Reit	$2.080	$1.350	$0.730	54.07%

Keppel DC REIT ended 2019 as the best performing REIT.

Like all REITs, Keppel DC REIT's share price took a hit as the COVID-19 crisis rolled-in. Unlike all REITs, Keppel DC REIT price subsequently recovered very quickly and even exceeded its pre-COVID-19 price in as short as five weeks, one of the hallmarks of a good and strong REIT.

	IPO	IPO	Total	Price	%
	DATE	PRICE	DPU	30/06/20202	Change
KEPPEL DC	12th Dec 2014	$0.930	$0.373	$2.550	274.19%
	Total Return		CAGR		
	$	%	Total	%	
	1.9933	214.33%	2.9233	23.15%	

Keppel DC total return and CAGR since its IPO on 12 December 2014.

As at end-June 2020, Keppel DC REIT closed at $2.55. A perspicacious and shrewd REIT investor who has invested in Keppel DC at its IPO at $0.93 on 12 December 2014 would have enjoyed a massive capital gain of $1.62 or 274.19%. In terms of total return including all the dividends received, the total return would have been a scintillating $1.9933 or 214.33%. In terms of CAGR growth, the REIT would have delivered an astounding 23.15% growth! This means that you would double your investment capital every 3.5 years in Keppel DC REIT. Who says you can't make big money in REITs?

LESSON LEARNED

REITs that do well after asset acquisitions need not offer private placements at too sharp a discount to warrant success of financing the deal. Empirical evidence has shown that REITs which undertake private placements that lead to minimal dilution for existing shareholders can even decrease their gearing after successful acquisitions, a very rare feat. The share price performance thereafter will testify to the market appreciation of such deals.

LOOKING FORWARD – REIT ACQUISITIONS

Going forward, the lynchpin for REITs outperformance would lie in inorganic growth, particularly through asset acquisitions. REITs that make DPU- and yield- accretive acquisitions will be on investors' radar.

The S-REITs that will do well in future acquisitions will be:
1. Those with a strong acquisitions pipeline.
2. Those with strong sponsors that have shown that asset injections will be at win-win prices for both sponsors and shareholders.
3. Those with strong AEI potential and asset recycling potential.

Investors would be looking for acquisitions that are both DPU accretive and yield accretive. Smart REIT investors should always be wary of REITs that apparently undertake yield-accretive acquisitions, but are in actual fact, non-DPU accretive after taking into account the timing and capital market conditions. Some managers excuse themselves that "capital market conditions have changed" to account for non-yield or non-DPU accretive acquisitions, but it is an excuse that should be frowned upon. It is a simple rationale – if you are paid handsomely to professionally manage the REIT, you should have the expertise or foresight to judge the timing of critical market operations which can have profound dilutive effects for shareholders.

LESSON LEARNED

Optimizing long-term capital allocation strategies is of utmost importance to REIT investors in picking the right REITs that can reap the investor millions in profits. The sagacious REIT investor should always demand better clarity on acquisition decisions made by the REIT manager, and how they are made. REIT managers should engage with their investors, even in the minutiae of such corporate decisions as they have a fiduciary duty to their investors.

Chapter 9

HOW I MADE MY MILLIONS IN REITS

In Frasers Centrepoint Trust's (FCT) latest 2019 Annual Report, I am listed as its top 16th Shareholder. In fact, I have been a FCT top-20 shareholder since its IPO at $1.03 in 2006 as shown in its first Annual Report in 2007. So, 2020 is my 14th year as FCT's shareholder, and a profitable one indeed.

FRASERS CENTREPOINT TRUST

Annual Report

TOP 20 SHAREHOLDER'S RANKING

	FCT STATISTICS OF UNITHOLDERS	
As shown in the Register of Unitholders - YAP CHONG HIN GABRIEL		
FINANCIAL YEAR#	TOP 20 SHAREHOLDER'S RANKING	NUMBER OF UNITS
FY2007	16th	800,000
FY2014	18th	1,585,000
FY2015	18th	1,500,000
FY2016	16th	1,700,000
FY2017	16th	1,740,000
FY2018	15th	2,120,000
FY2019	16th	2,120,000

#FCT Financial year end is 30 Sep

My rankings in various years in Frasers Centrepoint Trust annual reports.

I will devote this chapter to examining and sharing the reasons and circumstances of a REIT pick at the right price for a substantial stake, in this case how I built up my stake in FCT over the years. It is part of my philosophy that patience is an important element of REITs investing as you should wait till all the circumstances are right before making your million-dollar purchase in a REIT. Sit and Wait for the right timing might sound easy, but my experiences have taught me that might be one of the hardest things to do. Sit and Wait to invest big requires a different kind of psychographics, something that we try to impart in our REITs Quarterly and Master classes, all these decades

THE MARKET OFFERS VALUE, BUT YOU NEED TO KNOW WHEN TO SEIZE IT

When the Global Financial Crisis (GFC) hit in 2008, FCT's share price took a dive to as low as 47 cents. The share price practically collapsed from a $1.20 to $1.30 range to below 50 cents before stabilizing at around 60 cents towards end-2008 as the crisis reared its ugly head.

However, the fundamentals of the REIT were quite different to the share price direction. Despite a difficult year, probably the toughest ever for retail in the past two decades, FCT still posted NPI growth of 9.4% to $56.6 million and DPU growth of 11.3% to 7.29 cents in FY2008. Importantly, the REIT was able to navigate the GFC with its major mall Causeway Point posting NPI growth from $37.2 million to $39.6 million. Only Northpoint which was undergoing a $39 million AEI to integrate with its new wing Northpoint 2 to create a seamless 232,000 square foot mall, suffered a slight NPI drop from $14.7 million to $13.5 million. FCT NAV grew from $1.16 to $1.23 while its gearing dropped from 29% to 28%. Readers will note that FCT was able to almost measure up to all the performance and valuation metrics that we have in highlighted in Chapter 4 – Analysing REITs for Outperformance and Chapter 5 – How Much to Pay for a REIT? It is also important to note that FCT continued to eke out positive growth in DPU while navigating the GFC.

	FY2007	FY2008	FY2009	FY2010
DPU (cents)	6.55	7.29	7.51	8.20

FCT continued to eke out positive growth in DPU while navigating the GFC.

Thus, it was a no-brainer for me to buy FCT further as the share price went to as low as 47 cents. The great value that the GFC presented was just too much to go to waste if it was not seized upon. Great buying opportunities happen during a crisis, especially even more glaring if the fundamentals of the REIT had continued to improve during a crisis, which was the case for FCT.

LESSON LEARNED

The true colours of a REIT, like a person, and how good or bad it is, is most evident during a crisis. Good REITs can still strengthen their operational efficiencies and serve up steady fundamentals during a crisis. The smart and sharp investor should incorporate crisis management in his/her own investment process as crises are the best times to buy good REITs at dirt-cheap prices.

FCT share price staged a powerful rally post-GFC. It rallied throughout 2009 to close the year at $1.40. By April 2013, it had already crossed $2.20 and I started to take profits as my buy price was below $0.60 at end-2008. FCT share price continued to rise to as high as $2.34 on 3 May 2013. For every million shares, the profit was ($2.20 - $0.60) x 1 million = $1,600,000! Not bad for a holding period of just 4.5 years.

My premise for profit taking was not only driven by the huge price surge of 267% (including quarterly dividends, my total return was more than 300%), but by a few of the fundamental valuation benchmarks which we have shared in detail in Chapter 5. Many of the yield-based valuation measures of FCT have hit record highs as the share price crossed through $2.20. Moreover, in the previous financial year, FY2012, DPU growth registered a very good growth of 20.31% from 8.32 cents in FY2011 to 10.01 cents in FY2012. This was FCT's strongest DPU yearly growth since its listing in 2006. The growth was boosted by a full-year contribution of Bedok Point, which was acquired in FY2011.

I was of the view then that the phenomenal growth was an aberration and unlikely to be repeated. Thus, the take profit decision. Subsequently, I was proven correct as FCT's yearly DPU growth never came near to 20%. In fact, in the ensuing six years from FY 2014 to FY2019, FCT's highest yearly DPU growth never exceeded 4%. It registered an unexciting growth of as low as 0.42% in FY2019 to 3.75% in FY2015.

	FY 2011	FY 2012	FY 2013	FY 2014	FY 2015	FY 2016	FY 2017	FY 2018	FY 2019
DPU (cents)	8.32	10.01	10.93	11.19	11.61	11.76	11.90	12.02	12.07
DPU Growth Rate		20.31%	9.19%	2.38%	3.75%	1.29%	1.19%	1.01%	0.42%

I was proven correct as FCT's yearly DPU growth never came near to 20% after FY2012. In fact, in the ensuing six years from FY 2014 to FY2019, FCT's highest yearly DPU growth never exceeded 4%.

What goes up fast will also come down fast. Markets, by nature, can be fast and furious, like in the movies. This is also one of the tenets that we have been teaching in the past decade. The sharp and smart REIT investor should be able to recognize such conditions and act before the prices turn.

FCT subsequently collapsed to below $1.70 in January 2014. Investors were able to pile in at as low as $1.65 levels, which lasted for a month. This opportunity allowed me to buy back all and more of the same shares that I had sold just months back.

Come 2014, I was listed as the top 18th FCT shareholder with a total shareholding of 1.585 million shares. At year end-2014 closing price of $1.895, my holdings was worth more than $3 million.

A REIT IS AS GOOD AS THE KIND OF PROPERTY IT OWNS

It is easy to understand why FCT's price was able to climb steadily from the GFC through to 2014 if you have read through Chapter 4 in detail as FCT exhibited almost all the same characteristics that we highlighted in a good REIT. A good REIT is as good as the kind of property that it owns.

Operationally, FCT was able to deliver steady and consistent NPI growth from $80.05 million in FY2010 to $118.10 million in FY2014 on the same assets that it had at IPO, with the addition of Changi City Point. That translated down to the DPU which grew from 8.20 cents in FY2010 to 11.19 cents in FY2014. More importantly, while NPI grew by 47.53% over the 5-year period to FY2014, DPU grew commensurately by 36.46% during the same period, exemplifying a healthy growth at same-store sales. This same-store sales behaviour was also similarly exhibited by Parkway Life REIT as highlighted in Chapter 4.

I am always wary of REITs that grow their revenue and NPI, but not their DPU. REITs must realize that the two components of total return for shareholders are rising DPU and a rising REIT price. Moreover, the former is a huge lynchpin for the latter. It is a very simple principle, but investors will find this lacking in those REITs that have not been able to perform. Hence, this has become our paramount rule for seeking performing REITs in our investment classes all these years.

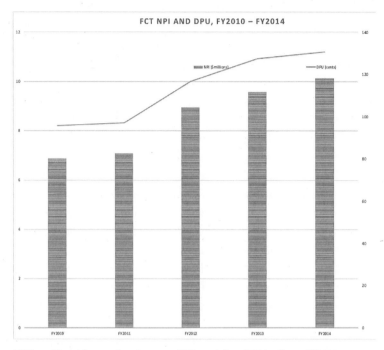

FCT was able to deliver steady and consistent NPI growth from $80.05 million in FY2010 to $118.10 million in FY2014 on the same assets that they had at IPO, with the addition of Changi City Point.

Once again, FCT also scored on many aspects per our checklist in Chapter 4. FCT's balance sheet metrics actually improved as it grew its asset base to $2.52 billion with its gearing ratio improved from 30.2% in FY2010 to 29.3% in FY2014. Its interest cover improved from 4.43 to 6.20. As highlighted in Chapter 4 – Analysing REITs for Outperformance, interest cover is directly affected by the income generating ability of the property and the interest expense incurred to finance the property. It is a good measure and when used together with the gearing ratio, it helped me to identify the strong financial position of FCT. This is further supported by its slow but steady rise in its book value or NAV from $1.29 to $1.85 over the corresponding period.

FCT is also a prime example of what we have been teaching in the past 31 years – A good REIT is as good as the assets that they have. It is still able to increase the key metrics of revenue, NPI and DPU growth over time on the same mix of assets if the assets are indeed good assets from the onset. REIT investors should not expect REIT managers to be able to perform any kind of magic in management as a REIT derives its value from the stream of income derived from its stable assets. It just has to ensure this happens, amongst other duties for which it has been paid.

Come August 2015, the Dow fell an unprecedented 1,000 points, the worst fall since a five-day drop in 2011. The tremor was felt in China as the Shanghai Composite collapsed by more than 10% in a week. Market concerns mounted after a key gauge of China's manufacturing activity tumbled to its nadir in 77 weeks. At the same time, the dollar weakened against other major world currencies such as the euro, British pound and yen, on speculation that the global market turmoil could push back a US interest rate increase.

That led to the third REIT market correction (the previous ones were in June 2011 and May 2013) in the decade. The FTSE REIT index fell 15.83% and FCT's share price ended the year rather weak at $1.845. That was the opportunity I was eyeing to increase my holdings further, which I did. Come 2016, FCT's FY2016 Annual Report listed me as the top 16th shareholder with 1.7 million shares.

LESSON LEARNED

The best time to buy is when the market punishes the REIT price, but the smart investor should know the REIT's quality of assets well enough to decide whether prevailing market prices are presently undervaluing its quality assets. The perspicacious investor should take note that invaluable bargains can be found during market corrections. And market corrections should be part and parcel of investing in a REIT.

VALUE OF A REIT = VALUE OF ITS UNDERLYING ASSETS +/- VALUE OF SPONSOR

By 2019, I was listed as FCT's top 15th shareholder with 2.12 million shares. Looking at its performance, NPI has continued to grow from $118.10 million in FY2014 to $139.3 million in FY2019. DPU in turn grew from 11.19 cents to 12.07 cents over the corresponding period. DPU growth was unexciting, but the REIT still managed to notch up positive growth Year-on-Year. On the surface, the 6.33% growth in 5-year NPI from FY2014 to FY2019 looks muted compared to the 47.52% growth from FY2010 to FY2014, a shorter 4-year period. However, if one looks at how FCT was able to navigate the huge supply of more than 5.2 million square feet, representing about 11% of island-wide stock as at 3Q2014 (close to a historical high in Singapore's retail history) of new retail space that came onto the market from 4Q2014 to 2018, the growth was actually commendable. It exemplifies one of the key lessons that we have been expounding in our classes – good REITs can still grow their DPU, albeit at a slower pace, even in times of industry headwinds.

Of course, not all FCT malls were resilient in the face of record supply onslaught. Both Bedok Point and Anchorpoint suffered negative reversionary rentals and occupancies in FY2018. While both Causeway Point and YewTee Point saw positive reversionary rentals, their respective occupancies also dipped in FY2018.

Despite the headwinds, FCT's balance sheet metrics actually improved as it grew its asset base from $2.52 billion in FY2014 to $2.84 billion in FY2018. Its gearing ratio improved from 29.3% to 28.6% despite the big-ticket purchase of Changi City Point. Its interest cover improved from 6.20 to 6.25. Its NAV increased from $1.85 to $2.08.

As highlighted in Chapter 5, REITs are asset-heavy in nature, the book value (BV) or NAV serves as a good indicator of how much an investor is paying for the underlying net asset of the REIT at any moment in time.

The P/BV or P/NAV is a good measure to assess if the REIT manager is prudent in the allocation of shareholder capital. NAV or book value measures the current market value of the REIT's properties and if the REIT manager had been acquiring well, valuations of the underlying asset should steadily increase and show up in the NAV or book value. REITs whose shares trade at a premium to book value have a serious competitive advantage as they can continue to buy or develop assets to grow their portfolios. This was clearly evident for FCT as it navigated one of the toughest periods in Singapore's retail history.

By FY2019, I was listed as FCT's top 16th shareholder although I did not buy any more shares as FCT's share price roared from $2.17 to $2.81 at end-2019. FCT was the top 8th best performing REIT for 2019.

TOP-10 PERFORMING REITS	Share Price	Share Price	Price	%
IN 2019	31/12/2019	31/012/2018	Change	Change
Keppel DC Reit	$2.080	$1.350	$0.730	54.07%
Mapletree Commercial Trust	$2.390	$1.650	$0.740	44.85%
Ascendas India Trust	$1.550	$1.080	$0.470	43.52%
Mapletree Logistics Trust	$1.740	$1.260	$0.480	38.10%
Sasseur Reit	$0.885	$0.650	$0.235	36.15%
Mapletree Industrial Trust	$2.600	$1.910	$0.690	36.13%
Manulife	$1.000	$0.770	$0.230	29.87%
Frasers Centrepoint Trust	$2.810	$2.170	$0.640	29.49%
Keppel Pac Oak US$	$0.780	$0.610	$0.170	27.87%
Parkway Life Reit	$3.320	$2.630	$0.690	26.24%

FCT was the Top 8th Best Performing stock for 2019.

The performance of FCT has vindicated what we have taught on REITs –

Value of a REIT = Value of its underlying assets +/-
Value of Sponsor

Hand-in-hand, DPU and DPU growth are probably the most important considerations for any REIT investor. A REIT's ability to grow its DPU over time is essential for generating good long-term returns for its unitholders. FCT has clearly shown that a REIT need not undertake huge amounts of acquisitions to grow NPI and DPU for shareholders. In fact, investors would prefer REITs whose management are conservative and can consistently add value to its strong portfolio of assets and achieve consistent, higher NPI yield.

The *per unit* information of a REIT is more useful than merely looking at the REIT's overall performance as it takes into account any dilution that may have occurred during the period under study. Also, management can attribute any kind of reasons for underperformance, but for the smart REIT investor, the bottom-line DPU and DPU growth is the ultimate measure of a REIT's performance.

LESSON LEARNED

Markets will pay a premium for REITs that can deliver positive NPI and DPU growth, even without active acquisitions. Strong sponsors that undertake acquisitions with financing structure that are favourable to minority shareholders are an added plus. The other common factors amongst those REITs that outperform are those whose managers have consistently added value through rigorous and careful property management, and undertake smart AEIs that achieve good NPI yields.

VALUING MANAGEMENT COMPETENCE – QUALITATIVE EXERCISE AND ART TO BE DONE CONSISTENTLY

At GCP Global, we still manage money and invest in the old-fashioned way – while we use Artificial Intelligence programs to throw up inconsistencies and Big Data to ensure that we have a comprehensive view of all things REIT, we are also assiduously meeting up with the REITs CEOs and/or heads of investor relations on a quarterly basis to be updated on all operational matters over lunch or coffee.

As what we teach our students, if you are well-equipped to ask the correct questions of high quality, you will usually get good quality answers to help you in the investment decision process. This way is also one of the best ways to size up management competency; mentioned in textbooks, but hardly taught in real-life experience.

With respect to FCT, another good measure of management competence is the ability to grow its NAV per unit from S$1.27 in 2010, to $1.85 in 2014 and then to $2.21 in 2019. This is actually a big achievement for FCT as along the way, it has had to grapple with problems from Bedok Point. Improvements in NAV are very important indicators of performance for investors as they reflect in total, whether management had bought the asset on the cheap or whether management had been sharp and gotten a good price for the asset in a sale.

It is noteworthy that the gradual and consistent improvements in BV or NAV were achieved from almost the same set of assets, namely its six retail properties. These mirrored the gradual improvement in the appraised value of its assets which grew from $1.44 billion in FY2000 to $2.85 billion in FY2019. This steady growth was marked by gradual and consistent tightening of its capitalization ratios or cap rates. As elaborated in Chapter 5 on cap rates, an attractive REIT is one that derives good cash flows from the quality assets that it owns. Thus, the cap rate essentially tries to capture how attractive the property is in terms of the yield. The cap rate reflects the nature, location and tenancy profile of the property together with current market investment criteria. REIT investors should never expect REIT managers to be able to perform magic in management, but rather to manage in such a way so that the magic embedded in the assets owned can shine through.

LESSON LEARNED

Consistent and steady improvements in NAV are very important indicators of performance for investors as they reflect in total, whether management had bought the asset on the cheap or whether management had been sharp and got a good price for the asset in a sale. These will be mirrored by the gradual improvement in its asset value, marked by gradual and consistent tightening of the properties' capitalization ratios or cap rates.

GOOD ACQUISITIONS BY REITS – LYNCHPIN IN PRICE OUTPERFORMANCE

Acquisitions or the potential pipeline of acquisitions can send share price into a frenzy. We have always taught that good acquisitions undertaken by REITs can be a lynchpin to superb share price outperformance, especially if the new acquisitions come with outsized DPU accretive impact, as our detailed example on Keppel DC REIT has shown in previous chapters.

After a hiatus of five years, FCT embarked on a one-third acquisition of Waterway Point in Punggol for $433 million in July 2019. Waterway Point is a 4-storey suburban family and lifestyle shopping mall with NLA of 371,200 square feet. FCT subsequently increased its stake to

40%. But what was more exciting was that FCT also got a toe-in into the PGIM Real Estate Asia Retail Fund which owns other suburban retail assets like Century Square, Tampines One, White Sands, Tiong Bahru Plaza and Hougang Mall. PGIM Real Estate is the property business of PGIM, the global investment management arm of New York Exchange-listed Prudential Financial Inc.

Both acquisitions drove up the share price of FCT substantially. FCT exceeded the $3 price level in early-2020, a level that prompted me to sell a substantial portion of my stake. As elaborated in Chapter 5, I have used both qualitative and quantitative factors to decide when to sell. The latter are largely covered in both Chapters 4 and 5 as well as the narrative below.

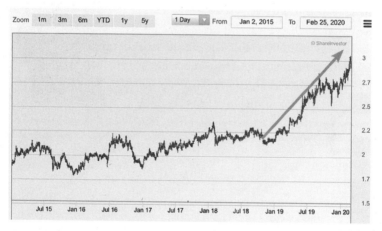

Best time to sell FCT after it has surged 38.25% in just 13 months! Source: ShareInvestor.

WHEN TO SELL YOUR REIT

Qualitatively, what prompted me to sell a substantial portion of my FCT above $3 in early-2020 (similar to what I did in April and May of 2013), after holding my stakes for six years, are as follows:

1. Price had risen too fast in a short period of time

FCT ended 2018 at $2.17. When the price crossed $3 in February 2020, it reaped me handsome gains. For instance, for every million of FCT shares, my net worth increased by ($3 - $1.70) = $1,300,000.

This substantial surge in FCT is unparalleled in the trading history of FCT since its IPO in 2006. Also, this surge was over a very short period of less than 13 months.

As in 2013, my premise for profit taking was not only driven by the huge price gain of 76% (including quarterly dividends, my total return was more than 100%), but by a few of the fundamental valuation benchmarks which we have shared in detail in Chapters 4 and 5. Many of the yield-based valuation measures of FCT have hit record highs while the various risks, as highlighted in Chapter 6, have also risen as the share price crossed through $3.00 to post new highs.

As a guide by comparison, Keppel DC REIT posted gains of 54.07% in 2019. This was already the largest % gain for any top REIT in any single year in the past decade!

2. Take profit when share prices have become over-stretched even when the fundaments are still strong

BEST PERFORMING REITS 2013–2019	Share Price 31/12/2013	Share Price 31/12/2019	Price Change	% Change	NAV 31/12/2019	P/NAV 31/12/2019
Mapletree Commercial	$1.190	$2.390	$1.200	100.84%	1.70	1.41
Mapletree Industrial	$1.345	$2.600	$1.255	93.31%	1.51	1.72
Mapletree Logistics	$1.040	$1.740	$0.700	67.31%	1.17	1.49
Frasers Centrepoint Trust	$1.770	$2.810	$1.040	58.76%	2.21	1.27
CapitaComm Trust	$1.450	$1.990	$0.540	37.24%	1.81	1.10
AVERAGE						1.40

Top five performing REITs in the past six years.

The above table was shown in Chapter 5 and reproduced here. It shows the top-five performing REITs of the past six years till end-2019. MCT, the top performer achieved a 100.8, 4% return over six years or a simple average of 16.81% per year. CCT achieved a 37.24%

COVID-19 struck and sent FCT's share price down to as low as $1.64, more than 42% down from the prices that I have sold in February 2020 at above $3. Needless to say, it was another great buying opportunity of a life time to buy back the FCT that I had previously sold. "Times like these are when fortunes are made", our tagline in the throes of the severe COVID-19 sell-down. Source: ShareInvestor.

return over six years, so FCT's huge 38.25% surge (when it crossed above $3) in just 13 months is indicative that the share price has overstretched, granted that the fundaments are still strong.

Locking in triple-digit returns in REITs is a patient, skilful process that tests your mental and psychological resolve, as much as an understanding of how the REIT's fundamentals and valuations have evolved and changed. It can be done, as I have done it with FCT, not once but twice, although it will be harder to come by in the future.

The sales which reaped me millions in profits, was as timely as it can get as less than a month later, COVID-19 struck, which sent FCT's share price down to as low as $1.64 on 3 April 2020, more than 42% down from the prices that I had sold. Needless, to say, it was another great buying opportunity of a lifetime and I bought back FCT in a big way. This exhilarating journey was shared real time in our various weekly Facebook Live sessions entitled Navigating the Current Crisis[1] with GCP Global student investors. As it turned out, our tagline throughout the crisis, "Times like this are when fortunes are made", emerged as an accurate prediction.

---

1   GCP Global, https://www.facebook.com/gabrielyap17/.

3. Never fall in love with a REIT

REIT investors often fall in love with a REIT. We have always advised our student investors to fall in love with their girlfriends or boyfriends before they tie the knot. Upon marriage, to learn to fall in love with their spouses again and again to enjoy eternal blissfulness, just as when they are dating. Love can, indeed, be sweet. However, when it comes to REITs, never follow this rule.

A REIT is as good as the income stream derived from its various assets. As investors, we should always check and counter-check to ensure that the REIT is able to increase the key metrics of revenue, NPI and DPU growth over time on the same mix of assets. If the REIT acquires, the same metrics apply while incorporating the acquisition process, as enumerated in Chapter 8. REIT investors should not expect REIT managers to be able to perform any kind of magic in management as a REIT derives its value from the stream of income derived from its stable assets. Thus, if the share price goes up too sharply relative to its historical performance and over a short space of time, be prepared to book in your millions in profits. There is always a time to buy back the same, if not more of the same stock, when the price corrects itself.

The "sell" decision in any investment process is always understated, but it is probably more important than the "buy" decision in determining the value of one's gain.

Chapter 10

POTENTIAL OF REITS AFTER COVID-19

The potential is tremendous.

REITs operate in a dynamic dimension that is evolving rapidly as epidemics, disruptive technology, developing legislation, evolving corporate governance and globalization continue to influence and lead changes in the world.

The REIT concept is gathering pace globally. There are now more than 38 REIT markets with a market capitalization of more than S$2.5 trillion as at 30 June 2020, up from S$1.1 trillion in 2010. Notably, the bulk of the increase in market capitalization in the global REITs market in the past nine years came from non-US REITs. Within the latter, Australia, Japan and Singapore have been some of the fastest growing REIT markets.

IPOs of Asian REITs have already grown strongly over the past decade with the total number of REITs growing from 50 to 796 by end-2019 as the market capitalization of the S&P Asia Pacific Ex-Japan index grew by more than 72%.

Whilst REITs have predominantly been a largely developed-market phenomenon so far, the past decade certainly has turned out to be a turning point where incremental and faster growth is likely to come from emerging markets, particularly Asia. And within Asia, the potential for REITs in Singapore, India and China look the strongest.

As elaborated in Chapter 2, the relative maturity of the different REIT regimes will likely affect the operations and how certain activities of REITs are conducted within a particular jurisdiction.

For instance, in the more mature or established REIT jurisdictions, fund raising comes at tighter spreads and faster speed as compared to nascent REIT regimes like Bulgaria, Brazil or Bahrain.

Where REIT legislation exists in Asia, different rules and regulations abound in the areas of maximum gearing, taxes, withholding taxes and the amount of greenfield development that a REIT can undertake. Many common areas do exist, which generates significant interest from new jurisdictions looking to use the REIT concept to monetize and deepen their respective property sectors. Underlying this drive and growth is the motivation to gain access to capital.

INDIA

IN-REITs are registered with the Securities and Exchange Board of India (SEBI) under SEBI (REITs) Regulations, 2014. The move by the Indian government to allow foreign investments in REITs and rationalization of the tax code paved the way for the first listing of an Indian REIT – Embassy Office Parks REIT in 2019. This was after a decade of investment in Indian assets by several foreign REITs, including Singapore-listed Ascendas India Trust. Separately, SEBI also authorized the framework for infrastructure investment trusts (InvITs), for revenue-generating infrastructure assets such as highways, warehouses, airports and roads for listing.

One lesson from the Indian experience is that while the regulations were first introduced in September 2014, the tax provisions were not attractive enough for the market to launch any REIT or InvIT as the stipulations in the legislation did not promote tax efficiency. This is a common problem that is being experienced in the Philippines as well as China, a potentially huge REIT market.

Sponsors and sponsor groups have to collectively hold a minimum of 25% of IN-REITs for at least three years post-IPO. Thereafter, there is a phase-down period, but sponsors and sponsor groups would still need to own at least 15% of the outstanding units of IN-REITs at all times.

Blackstone-backed Embassy Office Parks owns and operates a 33 million square foot portfolio of Grade A office parks and four city-centre office buildings in India's best-performing office markets of Bengaluru, Mumbai, Pune and the National Capital Region. In fact, this IPO took top honours as the largest listed, by floor space, office REIT in Asia when it listed in 2019.

The timing of the IPO was opportune as office demand in India is very strong, driven by a strong domestic economy, mainly from the IT and international outsourcing sectors. Strong demand for the IPO came from real estate funds, pension funds and sovereign wealth funds.

The IPO price of Embassy REIT was 300 rupees. The IPO raised 47.5 billion rupees (US$690.31 million). It has soared 46% to 486 rupees as at end-January 2020. However, COVID-19 brought about its major correction and it ended at 343 rupees as at 30 June 2020.

COVID-19 exemplified the dire need for capital in India's real estate market which is valued at close to US$190 billion at end-2019. Indian banks have hit their lending limits to the real estate sector. In fact, the majority of real estate deals in the past few years have involved a high level of participation from developers, private equity funds, pension funds and sovereign wealth funds.

THE PHILIPPINES

The Philippines is a market with strong fundamentals and while there has been REIT legislation in place since 9 February 2010 (yes, 10 years ago), there has been no REIT listing to date as rules governing minimum public ownership (at 67%) were too onerous and the tax (VAT at 12%) on asset transfers from developers to REIT vehicles was on the unattractive side.

Presently, taxes on VAT transfers have been slashed to 0% and it has been proposed that minimum public ownership be reduced to 33% to make it viable for REIT owners. This is on condition that the proceeds received by the sponsor/promoter are reinvested back to the Philippines within one year from the receipt of proceeds. Also, the requirement currently is that one-third or at least two, whichever is higher, of the members of the board of directors of a REIT must be independent directors.

The Philippine economy is one of the fastest growing, its population one of the youngest and it has some of Asia's major developers like Ayala Land, Megaworld, Filinvest Land and SM Prime. The prospects are tremendous.

On 24 April 2020, Ayala Land announced that it would launch a US$500 million REIT, known as AREIT, seeded with three office assets in Makati, Manila. It is expected to raise as much as 1.36 billion pesos in net proceeds that will fund future property investments. The Philippine Stock Exchange subsequently confirmed the listing of AREIT on 18 July 2020. The application came after the release of the Revised Implementing Rules and Regulations (IRR) of Republic Act No. 9856 or the Real Estate Investment Trust Act of 2009.

HONG KONG

Hong Kong REITs are authorized by the Securities and Futures Commission under the Code on Real Estate Investment Trusts. There are currently 10 REITs with a total market capitalization of about S$60 billion at end-2019. Six of these 10 REITs hold real estate predominately in Hong Kong while the other four REITs hold assets predominantly in Mainland China.

Hong Kong's first REIT listing was Link REIT which was spun off the Hong Kong Housing Authority in 2005 as a separate unit to house a number of its suburban shopping centres and car park lots.

It was one of the REITs that we emphasized as a strong buy to our student investors when it came up for IPO on November 2005 at a price of HK$10.30. Link REIT was one of the rare REITs then that had the scale and the corresponding quality of good assets, but was under-appreciated by investors at the time of the IPO.

Many of Link REIT's assets sit on top of the MTR or metro stations which make their locations close to ideal. Moreover, most of the malls cater to the surrounding population's necessity shopping, as opposed to tourists' discretionary spending. This makes the earnings and cash flows of such assets rock-solid.

The other bonus factor was that under the previous ownership of the government, the assets had had little investments and upgrading.

This led to under-rented properties which provided a great opportunity to investors.

All the new manager of the newly-formed Link REIT had to do was to invest further in quite logical asset enhancement initiatives (AEI), spice up the malls and they were able to increase rentals thereafter. In many cases, rentals soared by as much as 20% to 30% after the AEI.

Not surprisingly, from its IPO price of HK$10.30 in November 2005, Link REIT's share price rose to close at HK$80 at end-2019, a total return of more than 800% after counting the dividends, received twice-yearly, all these years.

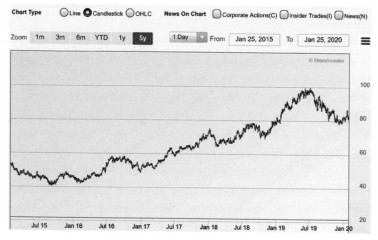

Link REIT rose from its IPO price of $10.30 in November 2005 to HK$80 at end-2019. Source: ShareInvestor.

CHINA
Present Difficulties
Mainland China began developing its own quasi REIT market in 2014. Nevertheless, quasi REITs are not true REITs in the traditional sense, as legal and tax arrangements are still being finalized. The development of REITs in China is faced with obstacles inherent to the legal system. At the heart of this stalemate is the specific legal definitions of the terms "trust" and "fund" within the context of Chinese law. REITs do

not necessarily have to adopt the form of trust or fund. Rather, a wide range of legal vehicles can be adopted via a contractual fund, collective trust or a corporation, for instance.

Thus, the current legal system is unclear and systematic regulations are not available. For instance, there is no definition of what constitutes a fund in the Securities Investment Fund Law, which is the only law governing funds presently. This would mean that it would be difficult for REITs to have legal title over the properties as they are not considered legal entities. Also, within the current trust law framework, it only regulates private issuance of securities by the China Banking and Insurance Regulatory Commission (CBIRC), not public issuance of securities. The latter is subject to laws and regulations outside the purview of the CBIRC.

The other problem is that the current tax regime imposes a high, or sometimes double, taxation which will impede dividend yields. In addition, developers or real estate companies would face a myriad of transaction costs like stamp duty, value-added (VAT) tax, land appreciation tax (LAT) in addition to corporate income tax. The holding of assets in a REIT vehicle is also subject to property taxes, VAT and corporate income taxes.

Thus, a common problem is the inefficiency of the Chinese tax collection system. This has resulted in great difficulty in determining the actual amount to be taxed versus actual collection of income. The operation of a REIT structure is related to a variety of transaction processes. While REITs may reduce the income tax levied on the fund, the multiple properties owned by the REIT are normally held by companies incorporated by trust which means that they are subject to corporation income tax. Furthermore, a transaction tax may arise from property transactions during a REIT restructuring process. All the required taxes payable under the current law will negate the positive effect of instituting a REIT structure which thrives on tax preferences.

Moreover, most of the taxes levied on asset transfers and rental incomes are paid to local provincial governments which are understandably reluctant to share such revenues with the national federal government.

Thus, for REITs to take a foothold in China, the current Chinese tax collection regime, the heart of the current stalemate, needs to be reformed and modernized.

Quasi REITs

In 2018, 14 quasi REITs started in China with a total valuation of RMB26.6 billion. Most quasi REITs are secured by retail and office properties, mainly located in Tier-1 and Tier-2 cities. They are the closest that China has to the types of REITs found in developed countries like the US and Europe and established Asian jurisdictions like Japan, Hong Kong and Singapore. Nonetheless, quasi REITs are more like asset-backed securities or quasi-debt structures rather than equity securitizations that provide shareholders with unitized ownership. Most quasi REITs are private and the only publicly traded quasi REITs are China Vanke and Penghua Fund Management when they were first introduced in 2015.

SINGAPORE

Reflecting Singapore's international outlook and leading wealth management hub status, more than 80% of S-REITs have invested in overseas assets, first in Asia Pacific then in China and now increasingly in Europe and the US in the past two years.

As highlighted in Chapter 2, understandably, due to limited investible local assets, most S-REITs that IPO since 2011 are predominantly with assets in foreign lands and even local REITs have been increasingly looking overseas for growth via acquisitions. However, growth via overseas acquisitions does not automatically equate to growth in REIT prices for REIT holders as overseas acquisitions should be analysed with greater scrutiny due to limited information and sometimes, a lack of independent sources for verification of certain trends and facts in relation to reversionary rentals, occupancies and tenants' veracity.

Again, as shown in Chapter 2, only 5 out of 22 REITs listed in the past decade (excluding those that were privatized or merged since) have posted capital gains compared to their IPO prices. The great thing is that some of the gains posted by the five winners are really outsized gains like Mapletree Commercial Trust's 119.32% and Keppel DC REIT's 174.19%. The negative thing is that 6 out of the 17 Losers registered losses of more than 40% as compared to their respective IPO prices. And, almost all REITs with 100% or near-100% overseas assets suffered negative losses.

For REIT buyers, this is very clear that to stay ahead of the game and be continuously profitable, one must always assess if the risk at IPO is commensurate with the expected returns that they are realizing. Media hype and the self-interest of IPO aspirants, underwriters and bankers should be understood and discounted by the smart REIT investor.

The perspicacious REIT investor should recognize from the onset that not all REITs fall into the same basket. Although REITs in general have outperformed the capital markets, it is imperative for the investor to be able to pick the right REITs for your portfolio for consistent and steady returns over the years and decades. Picking the wrong REITs can have huge negative impact on your profits and terminal wealth.

REITS IN THE COMING DECADE

REITs remain an attractive asset class with low volatility, consistent above-market dividend yields, and provide wide exposure to high-quality assets, across all asset classes in different jurisdictions. The long-term population and urbanization trend will continue to power the growth of REITs globally. This provides stable and realizable growth.

In all jurisdictions, REITs are creatures of the tax code, with aspects idiosyncratic to each country. Nonetheless, many commonalities exist which allow the sharp and smart REIT investor to transmute his/her knowledge gained from one market to another developing or nascent REIT market to generate and preserve wealth. A deep understanding of how REITs grow and their supportive financing structures needed to drive the growth are key to generating and enhancing wealth through REITs.

COVID-19 has brought on the problem of inconsistent and unreliable pricing of common equity in REITs for the sectors that have been affected by market pricing dislocation. However,

COVID-19 has probably set another dawn for low or near zero interest rates to persist for a long time. The last GFC sent interest rates down to near zero in 2008 and it was not until December 2015 when the Federal Reserve first raised interest rates again by 25 basis points, nearly seven years later. The next 25 basis points increase then came in December 2016 and it was not until 2018 that there was an increase of 75 basis points. This low interest rate environment is likely to persist for a few years in the coming decade, possibly reminiscent of the post-GFC experience.

This could underlie the continued outperformance of REITs vis-à-vis equities, bonds and other asset classes. In jurisdictions like China looking to launch C-REITs, this becomes most conducive as its real estate market has grown at exponential rates over the past three decades. The downside of the boom is the rising debt levels in the real estate market, leading to rising debt levels at the sovereign level. Real estate companies, developers, the central bank and the government would welcome the REITs structure as an alternative financing channel. Essentially, REITs can help the post COVID-19 situation as they help to release trapped equity from real estate to pay off debt and reduce overall leverage ratios.

Notably, based on past experience, major REIT markets seem to be born out of a crisis, be it financial or property-related in nature. They spring forth by bringing in liquidity and/or bringing down the debt financing levels. The US REIT market took off after the savings and loan crisis, leading to tax reforms in the 1980s while the Japanese and Singapore REIT markets emerged in the wake of the Asian Financial Crisis in the late 1990s.

For REITs, access to capital remains a critical priority and competitive advantage. The risk of over-reliance on capital markets, as elaborated upon in Chapter 6, has become more pronounced. REITs must and should recognize that only if acquisitions are both yield- and DPU-accretive, will the share price of the REIT perform. Only performing REIT prices will attract the serious, long-term and reliable investors.

The success of the REIT markets in Singapore and Hong Kong especially, will provide great potential for new listings. Moreover, with REITs legislation being revamped and finalized to meet many market participants' needs, new Asian markets for REITs like India, Philippines and China can become new magnets and supplement and cement Asia's reputation as a REITs base.

SUMMARY

Looking at the various REIT regimes, it is clear that for the successful development of a REIT market, the needed ingredients are:

1. Strong government support and initiatives
2. Strong central bank support and legislation
3. Clear and transparent tax structures
4. Ability of real estate groups to become strong sponsors
5. Ability of sponsors to have the right constituent assets
6. Access to the right constituent assets at the right price for investors
7. Strong corporate governance and transparency
8. An entrenched and well-informed investor class and capital market reach

The potential of REITs for investors, companies, regulators, central banks and sovereigns are indeed tremendous after COVID-19. If the past is a prologue to the future, you, the sagacious REIT investor, should always stay sharp and smart to continue making your millions in REITs.

ACKNOWLEDGEMENTS

From the deepest recesses of my heart, I want to thank my beautiful and lovely wife, Carmen. I thought I knew what happiness was before 50 years of age, but you have shown me what true and deep happiness entails. Your care and concern for others and our family makes me a happier happy person. For me, life begins in earnestness and sublime happiness after 50 with you.

I want to acknowledge the beauty, cries and smiles of my two daughters, Gabryna and Gabryane. Your coming into this world blessed us with God's greatest gifts and continuously make our daily lives so meaningful and filled with humour.

I want to thank my parents, Thomas and Mary, who taught and ingrained in me the virtues of hard work, honesty and integrity, even after 50 years.

I would like to thank my sisters, Geraldine and Gillian, for the years of taking care of each other and learning together the importance of family and love.

I would also like to thank my brother-in-law, Michael, for showing me the steadfastness and endeavours of a true educator, through love and patience.

My gratitude to Mr. Adrian Chui, CEO & Executive Director of ESR Funds Management (S) Ltd, who wrote my Foreword. I admire how you have transformed, steered and grown ESR-REIT since you took over the position of CEO.

The wonderful publishing team at Marshall Cavendish International (Asia) Pte Ltd, especially the affable and patient managing editor, Ms. Anita Teo.

All the 8,000 (and growing) student investors of GCP Global, who have attended our REITs and various investment classes in the past 31 years. Your constant questions and queries continue to keep me high on the thrills of REITs while avoiding the spills.

Last but not least, I want to thank God for giving me the wisdom, strength and energy to continue doing His Will, with even greater zeal after 50 years of age.

ABOUT THE AUTHOR

Gabriel Yap is well-known as the Investment Guru, having been regularly interviewed by Channel NewsAsia, Bloomberg TV, CNBC and Mediacorp Radio for the past three decades. He is the executive chairman of GCP Global, Asia's foremost educator in Real Estate Investment Trusts (REITs).

Gabriel hosted the inaugural Asian REITS Pinnacle Awards 2016 in Singapore and was chairman of both the Future of REITs Forum and the Fortune Times Asian REITs Pinnacle Awards 2016, and was the presiding judge for the Fortune Times Asian REITs Pinnacle Awards 2017. Gabriel also sat on the panel of judges for the prestigious Singapore Corporate Awards – Best Investor Relations 2017 and co-hosted the awards in 2019.

Gabriel has served as special advisor to pre-IPOs and IPOs of companies in various industries. He has lectured for 31 years. Some of the renowned institutions that he has lectured for include Asian Development Bank, Monetary Authority of Singapore, Institute of Banking & Finance, SGX, ASME, SIAS and Share Investors. He has also trained students for the grueling CFA course and has lectured and delivered academic papers internationally.

A successful stockbroker and investment banker, Gabriel retired in 2009 to devote himself to philanthropy and to share his knowledge of REITs.